CHRISTIANITY 2.0:

RENEWING A LIFE OF FAITH

AN ADULT STUDY FOR THE FALL

BOOK 1

Adult Education Series

Fall 2010

Office of Continuing Education
Lancaster Theological Seminary
555 West James Street
Lancaster, PA 17603
www.lancasterseminary.edu

Cover Design by James Siburt

ISBN 978-0-557-56829-1

Published in the United States of America

Editors: Bruce Epperly and Kathy Harvey Nelson

Editorial Assistant: April Bupp

DVD Videographer: Dan Bupp

Creative Director: James Siburt

TABLE OF CONTENTS

Word of Welcome

Day by day, as they spent much time in the temple, they broke bread at home and ate their food with glad and generous hearts, praising God and having the goodwill of all the people. And day by day, the Lord added to their number those who were being saved. (Acts 2:46-47)

The church is in a time of unprecedented transformation. While Christianity was once at the center of American life, now Christianity finds itself at the sidelines or margins of contemporary society. This is true for Christianity in general, but more challenging for those who call themselves moderate or progressive Christians. Our denominations are shrinking in membership and figures such as Rick Warren, Joel Osteen, and Pat Robertson dominate the public forum.

Christianity has always faced cultural and religious challenges. Although Christians are at the margins in our pluralistic age, the margins may also be the frontiers that lure us forward to new adventures and possibilities for faithful discipleship. Our situation today is similar to that of the first followers of Jesus, described in Acts of the Apostles. They were a small and struggling group, living in a pluralistic environment, facing persecution. They struggled to define themselves – Would the new faith focus solely on Jews or would it embrace the Gentile world? Would grace (Paul) or ethical behavior (James) be central to the emerging faith? No doubt, it felt like they were making it up as they went along at times, and perhaps they were, as they sought to discern the essential and inessential in the growing movement. They flourished, despite the challenges, because of their spirituality and commitment to one another.

Today, we need holistic approaches to Christian faith. Like the first Christians, we need to join theological reflection with prayer and social concern. Here at Lancaster Theological Seminary, our goal is to help congregations think theologically and connect theological reflection with daily life.

In this series, you will join head and heart to discern the

meaning of Christian faith for your life and congregation today.

Our study, Christianity 2.0, brings together thirteen members of the Lancaster Theological Seminary faculty to explore the many facets of Christian faith. We are united in our commitment to lay theological education, despite the fact that we speak in thirteen voices. Our goal in this study is not uniformity of style or perspective, but rather to present ways that Christians can understand their faith in the twenty-first century.

We welcome you to this holy adventure of theological reflection. We invite you to be open to God's Spirit in your congregation as you explore new ways to think and act as Christians.

May God bless you on the journey.

Rev. Bruce G. Epperly, Ph.D.
Publisher and Co-editor
Professor of Practical Theology
Director of Continuing Education

How To Use This Study Guide

We believe that this study will be most helpful to you and your fellow participants if you prepare for each session in advance. Each chapter will take thirty to sixty minutes to read. Take time to consider the themes being discussed, take notes, and raise questions. Each session is intended to be the starting point rather than the destination.

If you will be facilitating a class, read through each session in advance, and tailor your use of the questions to your particular congregation's needs. Don't hesitate to add or subtract questions or bring materials in (CD, DVD, movies, art work) to supplement the study guide.

We believe that theological study is important. So important, in fact, that it is important to us that you feel free to share your viewpoint and questions. In class, we ask you to commit yourself to creating a safe and hospitable environment for your partners in this adventure. There never has been one uniform Christian faith, so you should not expect or even desire for everyone to agree.

Remember that the early church was content with four different gospels, each of which gives a somewhat different perspective on the life and mission of Jesus. Further, New Testament scholars suggest that the Epistle of James was partly intended to emphasize ethical behavior among new Christians, some of whom had taken the Apostle Paul's focus on grace to an extreme, separating faith from ethics entirely. In the Old Testament, the Book of Job critiques the theology of Deuteronomy, which connected righteousness with health and wealth, and unrighteousness with sickness and poverty. Job was righteous and yet he lost everything.

And, of course, Jesus challenged his tradition's understandings of "clean" and "unclean" with the radical hospitality that characterized his ministry.

In the context of the many voices of faith, let your goal be to listen to the witness of others, to hear their vision of faith, where they have encountered Christ, and their struggles to be faithful. Let your light shine as you share your beliefs, but also let others share what is deepest in their understanding of faith. We grow in wisdom and stature and faithfulness by opening to God's wisdom in all of its diversity.

SESSION ONE

Faith as Trust: Toward a Holistic Understanding of Faith

Bruce Epperly

Leo Tolstoy tells a story of the encounter of a Russian Orthodox Bishop with three hermits as a way of understanding the holistic nature of faith. According to the tale, a Bishop was sailing from Archangel to the Solovétsk Monastery when he heard a story about three pious, but uneducated hermits who lived on a remote island in the Caspian Sea. He asked to be rowed ashore to meet them. When he saw them silently watching him on the beach, he greeted them and offered to teach them the essentials of Christian faith. The old men looked at each other smiling, but remained silent. "Tell me," the Bishop asked, "what you are doing to save your souls, and how do you serve God on this island." The second hermit sighed, and looked at the oldest, the very ancient one, who smiled and confessed: "We do not know how to serve God. We only serve and support ourselves, servant of God."

"But how do you pray to God?" asked the Bishop. "We pray in this way," replied the hermit. "Three are ye, three are we, have mercy upon us." And when the old man said this, all three raised their eyes to heaven, and repeated: "Three are ye, three are we, have mercy upon us!"

The Bishop smiled condescendingly at their simple theology as he replied, "You have evidently heard something about the Holy Trinity. But you do not pray aright. You have won my affection, godly men. I see you wish to please the Lord, but you do not know how to serve Him. That is not the way to pray; but listen to me, and I will teach you. I will teach you, not a way of my own, but the way in which God in the Holy Scriptures has commanded all men to pray to Him." And so he taught them the Lord's Prayer, telling them of God the Father, and God the Son, and God the Holy Ghost. "God the Son came down on earth to save us, and this is how He taught us all to pray. Listen and repeat after me: 'Our Father.'" And the first old man repeated after him, "Our Father," and the second said, "Our Father", and the third said, "Our Father." "Which art in heaven," continued the Bishop. The first hermit repeated, "Which art in heaven," but the second blundered over the words, and the third hermit could not say them properly. His hair had grown over his mouth so that he could not speak plainly. The oldest hermit also mumbled indistinctly. The Bishop repeated the words again, and the old men repeated them after him.

The Bishop sat down on a stone, and the old men stood before him, watching his mouth, and repeating the words as he uttered them. And all day long the Bishop labored, saying a word twenty, thirty, a hundred times over, and the old men repeated it after him. They blundered, and he corrected them, and made them begin again. The Bishop did not leave off till he had taught them the whole of the Lord's Prayer. When he left to return to the ship, he could still hear them reciting the Lord's Prayer.

The Bishop could not sleep as he thought about how pleased the hermits had been to learn the Lord's Prayer. He thanked God for having sent him to teach and help such godly, but simple, men. His feelings of satisfaction were interrupted by the sight of something white and shining on the bright path which the moon cast across the sea. "Was it a seagull, or the little gleaming sail of some small boat sailing after us?" the Bishop wondered. Suddenly, he saw something amazing: the three hermits running upon the water, all gleaming white, their grey beards shining. When they reached the ship, all three as with one voice, began to say: "We have forgotten your teaching, servant of God. As long as we kept repeating it we remembered, but when we stopped saying it for a time, a word dropped out, and now it has all gone to pieces. We can remember nothing of it. Teach us again."

The Bishop crossed himself, and leaning over the ship's side, said: "Your own prayer will reach the Lord, men of God. It is not for me to teach you. Pray for us sinners."And the Bishop bowed low before the old men; and they turned and went back across the sea.

Tolstoy's story captures the nature of faith as a holistic experience, involving body, mind, spirit, and relationships. Persons can have faith in God regardless of age, education, social class, or ethnicity.

Defining Faith. Recently, I asked a church school class how they defined faith. Their responses reflected faith as a whole person experience:

- "Faith is trust in God, regardless of what's going on."
- "Faith is hope in the unseen."
- "Faith helps me get through the day."
- "Faith gives me courage to reach out to strangers and work for justice."
- "Faith is believing that God is at work in my life."
- "Faith is knowing that God is with me, even if I don't always feel God's presence."
- "Faith is putting God first, and living for Jesus."
- "Faith is knowing that I'm forgiven."
- "Faith is affirming that God loves me and the whole world."
- "Faith is believing that God has a plan for my life."
- "Faith is opening to God's healing touch and sharing it with others."
- "Faith gets me off my feet and out into the world."

While these comments aren't exhaustive, they reveal something important about the nature of faith. Faith involves a trusting openness to God's presence in our lives. German-American theologian Paul Tillich defined faith as a person's "ultimate concern." Tillich believed that everyone has faith. While the nature of faith is similar in that it is the center of our lives, the objects of faith differ: the object of our faith, or ultimate concern, promises to give our lives meaning, purpose, and fulfillment and also asks us to sacrifice on its behalf. Tillich believed that the object of our faith can be known by how we answer questions such as: "What is the most important thing in the world to you? Where do you find meaning and purpose? What gives you fulfillment? What are you willing to sacrifice your life for?"

Because the stakes involved in having faith are high, Tillich asserted that doubt is an essential aspect of faith. The fact that we have faith is obvious; whether or not the object of our faith can fulfill us when the going gets tough may be a matter of doubt, rather than certainty. Tillich believed that only God can deliver what God promises: meaning and fulfillment in the midst of life's crises.

I must confess that when I first read Paul Tillich's *Dynamics of Faith*, my life was transformed and I found myself able to call myself a Christian once again. You see, having been raised in a conservative Christian environment where faith involved believing certain specific doctrines and where questioning and doubt were discouraged as faithlessness, I had difficulty calling myself a Christian when I could no longer believe the doctrines that I learned as a child. In opening to the possibility that faith is bigger than doctrine, I could once again claim to be a Christian with all my doubts; I could trust the teachings of Jesus, learn about Christian spirituality, discover my vocation as a pastor-professor, even though I still had pockets of uncertainty. This definition of faith still sustains me when I reflect on the immensity of our evolving universe of over one hundred billion galaxies and how little we can claim to know about God and God's creation. Tillich's definition of faith enables me to accept the reality of religious and doctrinal diversity both within and beyond Christianity.

Does Faith Make a Difference? In recent years, I have pondered the "faith factor," invoked by medical researchers, whose studies suggest that intercessory prayer, positive thinking, congregational involvement, service to others, and hopefulness can transform our bodies and relationships as well as our spiritual lives. In the spirit of the woman who came to Jesus, seeking healing from chronic bleeding, our faith can make us whole. In the spirit of both the mystical tradition and quantum physics, our faith can open us to new dimensions of reality as well as an influx of life-transforming energy. Faith and positive thinking can literally transform our responses to life's circumstances and, in some cases, the cells of our bodies. From my perspective, this does *not* mean that faith guarantees a positive health, employment, or relational result, but that our faith is a factor in our overall well-being and the well-being of others.

While faith is ultimately experiential and holistic in nature, faith ultimately constellates itself around an object of experience. For example, Peter could walk on water as long as he kept his eyes on Jesus. Faith is personal – it involves who, and what, we trust. But, how we understand the object of our trust can shape our lives in many, potentially conflicting ways. Friends, or Quakers, affirm that God's inner light is present in all human beings. Accordingly, Quakers treated indigenous peoples (Native Americans) of North America with respect and fairness, and opposed the enslavement of African peoples and the practice of slavery in England and the United States. In contrast, other Christians believed that God's omnipotence is the deciding factor in the question of who is saved and who is not, and who believes and who doesn't. The sovereign God inspired their sense of "manifest destiny" in the colonization of North America, South America, and South Africa. God had chosen them to colonize the Americas in the same way that God had given Canaan to the Hebrews. In this manner of thinking, persons who are not among the saved, or elect, do not deserve moral consideration. Thus, our understanding of the ultimate reality that faith affirms can cure or kill, liberate or oppress.

While the creeds of the church and theological reflection are essential to Christian communal experience, sometimes simple trust, such as that of the three hermits, can transform our lives and give us unexpected power. When he was asked to state the most important doctrine, Swiss theologian, Karl Barth, whose writings number thousands of pages, responded, "Jesus loves me, this I know, for the Bible tells me so." In a similar vein, when he was asked to name the most important truth of life, Albert Einstein responded, "whether the universe is friendly or not." Healthy faith says "yes" to life in its fullness and affirms God is good and the universe is ultimately on our side, despite appearances to the contrary. Faith becomes problematic when it suggests that we alone are blessed by God or possess the truth. Jesus affirms the universality of God's care in his statement that "God makes the sun to rise on the evil and the good, and sends rain on the righteous and unrighteous." (Matthew 5:45)

Faith Changes Our Lives. The philosopher Alfred North Whitehead noted that a person's character is formed according to her or his most deeply held beliefs. So faith itself includes both who we trust and how we understand the character of the one we trust. Our personal relationship with a God, whom we perceive as both loving and trustworthy, enables us to face tragedy with confidence that "it is well with my soul."

My own faith experience has been shaped theologically, spiritually, experientially, and musically. In one of the most challenging moments of my life, when our only son, just recently married, was diagnosed with a rare form of cancer, I was sustained by a chant and a hymn. Nearly every morning when I walked through Georgetown (Washington D.C.) where he was initially hospitalized, I chanted the Kyrie:

> Lord, have mercy upon me.
> Christ, have mercy upon me.
> Lord, have mercy upon me.

Although I was a theology professor, the only theology I could muster was a cry for help. In the spirit of the Psalmist, I placed my whole life and my son's in God's care, recognizing that we could not, on our own, bring about a healing. My faith was in a power and wisdom greater than mine, working through our prayers, medical expertise and technology, and the faith of a community. As his condition improved, I also turned to a hymn of thanksgiving from my Baptist childhood:

> Great is Thy faithfulness, O God my Father;
> There is no shadow of turning with Thee;
> Thou changest not, Thy compassions, they fail not;
> As Thou hast been, Thou forever will be.

> Great is Thy faithfulness!
> Great is Thy faithfulness!
> Morning by morning new mercies I see.
> All I have needed Thy hand hath provided;
> Great is Thy faithfulness, Lord, unto me!

> Summer and winter and springtime and harvest,
> Sun, moon and stars in their courses above
> Join with all nature in manifold witness
> To Thy great faithfulness, mercy and love.

> Pardon for sin and a peace that endureth
> Thine own dear presence to cheer and to guide;
> Strength for today and bright hope for tomorrow,
> Blessings all mine, with ten thousand beside!

We can sing, recite, and feel our faith. Perhaps, Erik Erikson was right when he asserted that the most important feeling we learn as infants is "basic trust," that the universe will respond to our deepest needs. Faith supports and restores this primordial trust so that we can act justly, lovingly, and boldly in the world, knowing that "nothing can separate us from the love of God in Christ Jesus our Lord." (Romans 8:39)

Faith Leads to Action. A holistic understanding of faith embraces heart, mind, and hands. With the Letter of James, we can affirm that "faith, if it has no works, is dead." (James 5:17) The Letter of James asserts that our faith is of little value if we neglect hungry and vulnerable persons. Faith leads to social transformation, according to the biblical tradition. As the prophet Micah affirms:

> What does the Lord require of you
> but to do justice and to love kindness
> and to walk humbly with your God?

Our beliefs shape our character and inspire acts of love. Martin Luther spoke of faithful people as "little Christs," whose vocation is to accept the grace and love that God has given them and pass it on to others through acts of service and mission.

In conclusion, faith is a whole-person enterprise. Directly or indirectly, it shapes the entirety of our lives. It enables us to be hopeful at the graveside. It inspires trust that gives us courage to challenge injustice. It awakens the energy of hope that can transform body, mind, and spirit. As our ultimate concern, faith shapes who we are, what is important to us, how we treat others, and what we hope for when all hope is lost.

Class Session

Spiritual Practice

Begin today's class with a time of silence, during which the leader reads Mark 5:25-34. Following the reading of the passage, take a few minutes to reflect in silence on the word, phrase, or image that "speaks" to you today. (The goal is not analysis, but listening for God's word in the scripture passage.) After a few minutes of silence, share as a group the words or images that spoke to you.

Questions for Discussion

1. On page 12, several definitions of faith are listed. Which definition of faith best reflects your understanding of faith? Would you add your own definition to those presented by the author?

2. Paul Tillich describes faith as "ultimate concern," which centers our lives, asks for ultimate sacrifice, and promises ultimate reward. In considering Tillich's definition of faith, consider the following questions:

- What do you think of his definition of faith?
- Is God the only object of faith that we have? Looking at your life and others' lives, do we have just one or many objects of faith? What other aspects of life ask for ultimate sacrifice?
- If your house were on fire, what would be the most important thing to take with you?
- If your church were on fire, what would be the most important thing to take with you?

3. Looking at your life, when has your faith gotten you through a difficult time? How was your faith helpful?

4. Medical researchers speak about the "faith factor." In light of the passage from Mark 5:25-34, what do you think of Jesus' comment "your faith has made you well?" Where have you seen faith make a difference in areas of health and illness?

5. One of the theses of the essay is that what we believe (the character of the object of our faith) can shape our ethical behavior and

attitudes toward others. It was suggested that two belief systems (the affirmation that God is present in all persons and the belief that God chooses some to be saved and others to be damned) had ethical consequences in terms of treatment of non-Christians. What do you think of this thesis? Where have you seen persons' faith reflected in their relationships and ethical behavior?

6. James 3:17 proclaims that "faith, apart from works, is dead." How do you understand the relationship of faith and action? In light of Micah 6:8, how might our faith shape our social responsibilities and political lives?

7. This essay notes two hymns that were important to the author — the Kyrie and "Great is Thy Faithfulness." In your faith journey, what hymns have been important to you? How have they shaped your life?

Concluding Prayer. Meister Eckhardt asserts that "if the only prayer you can make in your entire life is 'thank you', that will be enough." In conclusion, as a group, reflect on those aspects of your life for which you are thankful. For what aspects of your congregation are you grateful? Conclude by singing "The Doxology."

NOTES:

SESSION TWO

Faith As Belief: Fear No Doctrine (Or At Least Not All Of Them)

Lee Barrett

These days the concept "Christian belief" often gets exceedingly bad press. The suggestion that Christianity may involve a network of "beliefs" or "doctrines" is greeted with amused disdain or vehement hostility. Surely, it is alleged, Christianity is a matter of the heart, or perhaps the hands, but certainly not the head. Doctrines, it is claimed, are abstract, irrelevant propositions valued only by reactionary fundamentalists or ivory-tower academics. Even more damningly, talk of "beliefs" or "doctrines" is heard as suggesting rigidity, authoritarianism, and institutional meddling in the interior spiritual life of autonomous individuals.

Much of this hostility toward the belief component of Christianity is understandable, for all too often Christians have indeed separated the head from the heart and the hands. Christians have sometimes talked as if the Christian life were merely a matter of saying "yes" to certain officially sanctioned sentences. After the Reformation, some Christians did identify "faith" with an individual's assent to orthodox theological propositions. Moreover, in Christianity's history animosity and even violence have been spawned by debates about doctrinal rectitude. By the late sixteenth century, Protestants vilified Roman Catholic teachings, Lutherans condemned many Reformed doctrines, and everyone denounced Anabaptist convictions. As a result, many sensitive

Christians from John Locke to John Shelby Spong have suspected that the concern for right belief is a primary source of diabolic discord rather than a font of Christian concord.

Consequently, according to many Christians, a focus on spiritual experience should displace the emphasis once given to beliefs. The influential theologian Friedrich Schleiermacher, famously distinguished the roles of thinking, doing, and feeling in the religious life, and argued for the foundational status of feeling.[1] By so doing, Schleiermacher inadvertently generated an unfortunate way of dissecting faith. According to a popularized version of his approach, our espoused declarations of belief are merely efforts to express an underlying depth dimension of experience. According to this view, a self-identical experience of the sacred undergirds all Christian denominations and traditions. For example, some Christians may declare God to be the Almighty Lord of the cosmos, and others might define God as the vital energy that pervades the cosmos, but at their core these assertions are just different ways of giving voice to the same preverbal interior feeling of being sustained by some mysterious reality. From this perspective, the contents of our heads may be different, but the substance of our hearts is the same.

This picture is misleading. At a recent ecumenical meeting of Roman Catholics, Presbyterians, Methodists, Lutherans, and UCC folks one well-intentioned soul announced that the seeming doctrinal differences among the participants did not really amount to anything, because down deep they all shared the same experience of God's presence. However, as the conference progressed, it quickly became apparent that the existence of the alleged experiential common denominator was highly dubious. The Catholics talked about an almost erotic yearning to behold God's beauty, the Presbyterians described a feeling of being fascinated and terrified by God's glory, and the Lutherans confessed to a sense of being consoled by God's mercy. Moreover, each complained that

---

1Friedrich Schleiermacher, *On Religion: Speeches to its Cultured Despisers* (New York: Harper, 1968).

they could not even imagine the experience that the others were describing. Of course, these divergent experiences of God are not mutually exclusive, and all may well be equally significant, but at the affective level they are certainly different. Fear and trembling is not the same experience as serenity. Not surprisingly, the different experiences described by the individuals correlated with the divergent theological traditions from which they hailed. Perhaps it is not the case that Christians use different words to express the same underlying experience; perhaps more frequently they use the same words to indicate very different experiences.

Other Christians have disparaged "beliefs" or "doctrines" in order to lift up the foundational role of righteous action in the world. In their view, Christianity is not primarily a matter of the head, nor even of the heart, but rather of the hands and the feet. It does not matter what a person believes, it is sometimes alleged, as long as the person sincerely works for justice. For such people, ethical action in the world rather than theological convictions provides the foundations for the faith. As early as 1925 the Universal Christian Conference on Life and Work was advocating the slogans "service unites while doctrine divides" and "deeds over creeds." It is no wonder that many devout church members are inclined to reduce the faith without remainder to charitable actions or to ill-defined notions of social justice.

This divorce of action and belief is also unwise. A few years ago a Protestant congregation, rent with internal strife concerning the significance of Jesus, attempted to achieve unity by refocusing its energies on communal action in the world. Most of the congregants enthusiastically endorsed this strategy. Surely, they reasoned, down deep all Christians have an intuitive sense of what loving their neighbors involves. However, it quickly became clear that different segments of the congregation entertained incompatible understandings of what a commitment to justice would look like. For some, justice entailed a redistribution of opportunities and resources to economically disadvantaged segments of the population. For others, justice meant the maximization of individual freedoms through the elimination of governmental regulation of economic life. For yet others, justice meant the enactment of allegedly Christian principles in the public square. In other words, it became clear that different subcultures within the congregation entertained wildly divergent beliefs about the very nature of justice.

Perhaps there is no raw experience of God and no pure intuition of justice upon which Christians can base their lives. Beliefs about what counts as an experience of God or what constitutes justice inevitably enter the debate. Perhaps religious experience and social action are vague and directionless unless they are shaped by beliefs. The zeal with which many contemporary Christians ignore "doctrines" may be tragically self-defeating and, for our religious life, ultimately suicidal.

This widespread discontent with talk of "doctrines" is rooted in a misconception of what doctrines really are and how they function in the Christian life. Actually, "doctrines" are indispensable for human living; no one can act or feel in a coherent way without them. All of us entertain beliefs about the way things are in the universe. We may not be able to articulate what those doctrines are, or even be consciously aware of them. Nevertheless, all of us make decisions, formulate plans, succumb to fears, and cherish hopes that are based on sweeping assessments of what the world is like. To give a very ordinary illustration, I believe that I should take my car to a service center for its mandatory annual inspection. I do this because of a complex network of background convictions that I hold. I assume that keeping my automobile in functional order will contribute to my well-being and make life safer for other drivers on the highway. I also assume that the state regulations about inspections should be observed, for obedience to them is in everyone's best interest. I assume that the state law is not a tyrannical imposition that trammels my autonomy. Even more basically, I assume that care for my automotive safety is an appropriate response to the gift of life that I have been given by God, and is an exercise of the love for my neighbors that Christ has mandated. For me, these vague and usually unspoken convictions function as doctrines, guiding my behavior and shaping my emotions. All of us have core convictions that function as a sort of lens through which we view the world. These core convictions, which can be called "doctrines," lead us to regard some sorts of behavior as being suited to the way things are, and other sorts of behavior as being out of alignment with reality. They also lead us to feel certain emotions rather than others and even to harbor certain long-range hopes and fears. If I believe that pit-bulls are vicious and potentially lethal, I will be inclined to experience terror when I behold a froth-flecked pit-bull bounding toward me. I will also be inclined to engage in certain behaviors, perhaps screaming or fleeing as fast as I can. Our beliefs thus serve as directives to act and feel in certain ways, and as boundaries that demarcate appropriate feelings and responses from inappropriate ones. Consequently, doctrines are not just cognitive propositions dispassionately entertained in the head, but are rules governing the well-springs of feeling and action. Doctrines make possible thoughtful passions and passionate thoughts. An admission of the importance of "doctrines" does not devalue the importance of experience and action. The holding of beliefs about the nature of God does not detract from the intensity of personal experience or the zeal of commitment to transformative action. The heart and the hands need not disparage the head.

To understand a doctrine is to know how it impinges upon daily living. If I say "I am a firm opponent of the unregulated free market economy," but enthusiastically oppose legislation to monitor business practices or tax corporate profits, I probably do not really know what "free market economy" means. If I do not even know what it means, then I cannot possibly either doubt it or believe in it. To believe in a Christian doctrine involves much more than affirming a statement from a creed; belief includes a commitment to cultivate certain actions and feelings. For example, to declare that God is sovereign is to say that the uncertainties of this precarious life should be faced with courage and confidence. It is also to say that no earthly power should be unconditionally obeyed. To affirm that God is a Trinity is to claim that the individual should cultivate gratitude for the gift of life, take comfort in the good news of reconciliation, and to nurture the extravagant hope that the yearnings of all creatures will somehow be satisfied. "Beliefs" or "doctrines" have an imperative force, stipulating how an individual ought to think, act, and feel.

The attitudes, dispositions, and ways of experiencing life that constitute the Christian faith are not generic feelings that naturally well up in people, but are components of a specific way of life with a particular morphology. For example, Christian hope is not a Pollyanna-like attitude that every cloud has a silver lining, but is a much more specific expectation that God can bring reconciliation out of sin, liberation out of oppression, and life out of death. Christian love is neither a romantic attraction nor the warm, fuzzy familial feeling of being gathered around the Thanksgiving table. Rather, Christian love is an unstinting concern for the well-being of others, friends, strangers, and enemies; it is a reckless concern for others that is willing to dethrone the imperious demands of self-protective and self-aggrandizing ego. It is a love that is prepared to suffer and rejoices in emptying itself.

Because doctrines have a normative force, they are not the products of personal preference or individual invention. Doctrines are communal, public, and sharable. They are the implicit rules that structure a community's way of living and being. They are often so basic and pervasive that their presence remains undetected. Doctrines have been compared to the grammatical rules of a living language that make it possible to string words together in sequences that convey public meaning. They have also been likened to the rules of a game, rules that prevent the game from degenerating into a free-for-all of arbitrary actions. In chess, the proposition that the bishop moves in a diagonal line has the status of a doctrine; it is so integral to the playing of the game that its violation would make the formulation of strategy impossible. Without commonly shared doctrines, communities could not exist at all.

Some doctrines are absolutely foundational for a community's identity and way of life. For example, congregational life is predicated on the assumption that differences of opinion about a church's policies should be resolved through a prayerful exchange of viewpoints rather than by bloodshed. Local church life could not proceed if congregational factions habitually pulled knives on one another. In this way some doctrines serve as the tacit presupposition of everything that a community does. Such doctrines as the Trinity and the incarnation have historically functioned that way for Christianity. Foundational beliefs like these have not sprung up over night, nor are they the products of passing fads. These basic teachings have been practiced for a good while, so long that they have become second nature and taken for granted. Even the revision and modification of doctrines, actions that occur with regularity in a community's history, require the community's general perception that the novel elements are natural extensions of the trajectory of its convictions.

Most doctrines are usually left unstated, simply being implicit in the way that a community ordinarily does things. However, sometimes doctrines need to be overtly articulated, particularly when a community does not know how to proceed in the face of novel challenges that undermine business-as-usual. Such perplexity can stimulate a reexamination of the community's basic principles in order to discern how they could be applied to new situations. Accordingly, our spiritual ancestors developed catechisms, creeds, and confessions because they feared that the Christian life would lose its distinctive shape unless its central themes were publicly acknowledged and affirmed.

A doctrinal heritage need not lead to stagnation, as many contemporary people so deeply fear. Core convictions do not necessarily engender rigidity or fossilization. Nor does the willingness to heed the testimony of a tradition necessarily spawn a servile subservience to the authority of the past. On the contrary, the appropriation of a convictional tradition is a prerequisite for any genuine progress. Without a particular orientation, we would have no perspective from which to survey the contemporary scene and would certainly have nothing coherent, much less novel, to say. A doctrinal tradition is not the mechanical repetition of a static formula. Rather, a tradition is a community's historically extended conversation about the way its basic convictions should be enacted by new generations. Within a doctrinal tradition's trajectory there is ample freedom to explore, innovate, and even argue. For example, Wesleyans continue to debate what "holiness" means for contemporary life, and Presbyterians continue to explore what the "sovereignty of God" may mean for the twenty-first century. To participate in any tradition is to pursue a theme, inherited from the ancestors, into uncharted and sometimes contested territory.

In the midst of the current cacophony of cultural voices, it may be more important than ever to encourage a lively discussion of our basic Christian convictions. The church may need to be increasingly vigilant that the essential shape of its faith is not obscured by consumerism, the entertainment industry, and political ideologies. Perhaps now it is especially imperative to clarify what really is the "good news" that Christianity can offer a hurting, broken world. Christianity, we must remember, dares to proclaim certain audacious convictions: that love does beat at the heart of the universe, that justice will be triumphant, that reconciliation is deeper than alienation, that death is not the final word, and that a joy awaits us that cannot be imagined. Christianity makes specific claims about where we come from, why we are here, and what we can hope for. These convictions, rather than our piety or our programs, are the food that can feed our souls.

Class Session

Spiritual Practice

As you prepare for the study, the leader will read John 20:24-31. Following the reading, focus on the word, image or phrase that "speaks" to you today. After a few minutes of silence, share your discoveries with the group.

Questions for Discussion:

1. Fill in the blank in the following sentence: "Life is like a _____." Meditate on your answer, exploring what it may reveal about your own actual core beliefs about life.

2. Write a brief statement of your own faith, describing what is essential to your understanding of God, the world, humankind, sin, and salvation. Compare it to a recent declaration of faith by your own denomination. (For example, Presbyterians might want to examine "The Brief Statement of Faith," and UCC folks might want to consider the "Statement of Faith of the United Church of Christ.")

3. After considering as a group what is essential to Christian faith, reflect on what is inessential in your understanding of Christian faith, that is, what is optional or a matter of indifference?

4. Make a list of your deepest hopes and fears, the ones that really inform your life. Then ask yourself what they may imply about your beliefs concerning God, human nature, salvation, etc.

5. The author presents a strong case for the current disillusionment surrounding doctrine. What is your understanding of "church doctrines" and their value in light of your faith/belief? Do you find doctrinal beliefs to be more divisive or more unifying? Give an example to support your position.

6. The author presents a view that leads us to believe that, "the contents of our heads may be different, but the substance of our hearts is the same." In your experience, is this true? Is "God" the same, as understood by folk coming from varying doctrinal tradi-

tions? If you note some differences, are they mutually exclusive or really insignificant in the life of faith?

7. Some folk believe the most important part of the life of faith is that which spurs us to action. How does belief shape your understanding of religious experiences and social action?

8. Our author reminds us that, "To believe in a Christian doctrine involves much more than affirming a statement from a creed; belief includes a commitment to cultivate certain actions and feelings." How well do you think you know and understand the creeds of the church? Are there any creeds that your group needs to revisit?

9. How can your congregation and you personally find new passion for faith as you explore your doctrinal positions and faith creeds?

Conclude with a prayer of gratitude for those who have gone before us and taught us the faith. Take time to mention mentors, teachers, theologians, and pastors who have shaped your understanding of Christianity.

NOTES:

SESSION THREE

Reading the Bible: What's at Stake?
Julia M. O'Brien

What relevance does the Bible have for contemporary life? Does the church still need this ancient document? What about other arenas of life? Does the Bible belong in the court room, the science lab, the hospital ethics statement, and/or the bedroom? If the Bible is relevant, how is it relevant? What principles should guide its application to the present? Are the words on the page self-evident? Or is biblical interpretation always more complicated than a simple reading might suggest?

Conflict in Interpretation

All of us know that the answers to these questions range widely. Conclusions about "the biblical position" on abortion, assisted suicide, stem-cell therapies, the Israeli-Palestinian conflict, and the future of the planet generate debate not only on a national and international scale but also within our churches and our families. Many denominations know all too well that discussing the Bible's relevance to matters of human sexuality can cause conflict and even fracture. Many families have struggled to agree about how and how much the Bible should guide decisions regarding death—the role that doctors should play and the details of the burial and funeral.

At least in the United States, it's common to sort all positions into one of two categories. Perhaps because we have been socialized into a two party political system, we often label a stance as either conservative or liberal; as either a literal interpretation or something "looser"; as either religious or secular. The reality, of course, is far messier. Interpretations of the Bible rarely fall into neat categories. "Liberals" sometimes read the Bible's appeals to justice quite literally, while "conservatives" sometimes explain a given biblical instruction within its ancient context. Some secularists rail against the dangers of the Bible, while others believe it can provide valuable ethical guidance.

Nothing New Under the Sun

Disagreements about the Bible are nothing new. In fact, they stretch far back in history, as far we can see. In the 1920's, the famous Scopes Monkey Trial debated whether the account of creation in Genesis 1 should be read literally and thus as refuting Charles Darwin's theory of human evolution. Several decades earlier, the women's rights advocate Elizabeth Cady Stanton insisted that women will never make significant political gains as long as the Bible is used against them: in the Women's Bible, she and others reinterpreted the stories of Eve and Esther and the writings of Paul to challenge traditional teachings about women's inferiority and submissiveness. In the nineteenth century, both slaveholders and abolitionists defended their positions by appeals to the Bible: the former pointed to the acceptance of slavery in Exodus, Deuteronomy, and Paul's letters, while the latter lifted up the general biblical principles of equality and justice. Yet earlier in 1293, King James of Aragon ordered the Jewish philosopher Nachmanides to debate a Dominican friar on the question of whether the Old Testament confirms that Jesus is the Messiah.

Differences in interpretation are even reflected in the Bible itself. Acts 15 records a disagreement about whether basic tenets of Judaism are binding on Gentile Christians. The gospels of Matthew and Luke both quote Isaiah 9:2 but apply the words to different phases of Jesus' ministry: according to Matthew 4, Isaiah's statement that "the people who walked in darkness have seen a great light" was fulfilled when Jesus began his ministry in the Galilee, while according to Zechariah's speech in Luke 1 the Isaiah passage foretells John the Baptist's role in God's plan of salvation. Old Testament documents themselves show one text reinterpreting another: the claim in Jeremiah 29:10 that the exile will last 70 years is updated in Daniel 9:24 to signify 70 weeks of years--that is, 490 years. Most Christians are familiar with the vision of Isaiah 2:4 in which swords will be beaten into plowshares, but not with its opposite in Joel 3:10, which anticipates that plowshares will be beaten into swords.

Clearly, the meaning of biblical passages has never been simple. People have been interpreting the Bible—and interpreting it in different ways—since the time of its writing.

What to Do with Difference

The question facing Christians is what to make of this diversity and how to respond to it. Are differences about the relevance of Scripture resolvable? If so, what criteria can we use to decide on good interpretation? If our differences are not resolvable, how then can we worship, live, and work together as people of faith?

Just as interpretations of the Bible have varied over time, so too have responses to the differences in interpretation. For much of Christian history, disagreement over Scripture has been treated as a problem that needs to be solved: particular methods of study or particular principles of application have been advanced as the "right" way to read the Bible.

Apply the rule of faith.

In most Christian communities until the seventeenth century, "correct" interpretations of the Bible were defined as those that undergirded the orthodox teaching of the church. Scripture was read as corroborating the traditions of the faith, as passed down through faithful witnesses. For example, the church's affirmation that Jesus is Messiah became the lens through which the Old Testament was to be read; the prophets in particular were mined for what they might reveal about the life, death, and resurrection of Jesus (rather than for their significance to their original readers). When on first reading a biblical passage appeared to fall short of Christian standards, church interpreters offered alternative ways of reading that produced more favorable results. For example, the third century bishop Origen insisted that Christians should not take Psalm 137's ending call for dashing enemy children against rocks literally but instead as an instruction to dash one's passions against the hard truths of reason.

Over the centuries, other criteria have been used to determine correct interpretation. According to Augustine in the fifth century, all correct interpretation must adhere to the "law of love"; according to early Anabaptists, an interpretation is valid only if it undergirds Jesus' teaching of nonviolence. In these and countless other cases, the standards for "correct" interpretation are doctrinal and/or ethical: do they promote right thinking and action (as defined by the interpreter)?

Apply the law of logic.

The seventeenth and eighteenth centuries marked a significant shift in biblical interpretation, one spurred by major developments in science and philosophy. During this period, often called the Enlightenment or the Age of Reason, intellectuals in Europe and the U.S. touted the value of human reason to discern how the world and its creator worked. Convinced that the physical world and human nature follow unchangeable natural laws, they argued that human logic provides the best criterion for accurate biblical interpretation. This approach, usually called Historical Criticism, is explained in greater depth in the next chapter but most contemporary Christians are familiar with its primary claim: to determine what a biblical passage means we must learn what it meant in the past-- when it was written and what its ancient human author intended to say.

For those committed to this approach, the ancient meaning determines how a passage can—and cannot--be applied to the present. If the author of Romans 1 was not referring to consensual same-sex relations, then the passage has no bearing on the church's response to homosexuality. If the author of Revelation was referring symbolically to political events during the Roman period, then this book should not be treated as a blueprint for

Jesus' return. Early adherents of this method claimed that it was more objective than earlier interpretation. Meaning was determined by rigorous historical, literary, and sociological study rather than traditional beliefs. Their method, they claimed, allowed that the Bible could speak to the church rather than for the church.

These two approaches, church readings and historical critical methods, are often pitted as opposites. But while they do come to the Bible with different assumptions and produce different results, both advance criteria for proper interpretation. One insists that the Bible be read according to the "rule of faith" and the other insists upon "the rule of reason," but both insist on a rule. Because patristic and medieval interpreters spoke of Scripture's multiple levels of meaning (literal, typological, allegorical, and mystical), they are often described as open to diversity of interpretation. These levels of meaning, however, were seen as different routes to the same truths about God and God's church; no reading of Scripture on any level challenged the teaching of the church. Historical critics had their own orthodoxy, too. Even though they did free interpretation from the control of the clergy, their definitions of logic guaranteed that all conclusions about the Bible would conform to their own naturalistic worldview.

Embrace—and take responsibility for—the diversity.

By the late twentieth century, many people no longer shared the Enlightenment's confidence in human reason and objectivity. Brutal and on-going wars and genocides; well-publicized scandals involving politicians, clergy, and journalists; and greater awareness of the cultural and economic divides between people created a climate often called "postmodern." In this understanding of the world, objectivity is impossible; all claims to truth reflect a perspective. That perspective is not simply a matter of personal preference but rather is shaped by social and cultural institutions. A white middle class English professor sees the world differently than the woman who grew up in a Palestinian refugee camp during two intifadas.

For this reason, biblical scholarship in the past three decades has placed new emphasis on the role of the interpreter in determining meaning. Meaning isn't found simply in a creed (traditional Christian interpretation) or in an author's intention (historical criticism): it emerges from the interplay between the text and culturally-shaped readers. Many recent publications in biblical studies reflect this concern with the identity and interests of interpreters. The introductory volume of the New Interpreter's Dictionary of the Bible, for example, contains six articles on reading from particular social locations, such as "Reading the Bible as African Americans" and "Reading the Bible as Women."

Some postmodern approaches treat all interpretations as equally valid. Since all interpretation is based on one's social location and since there's no "right" social location, then there can be no "right" interpretation of the Bible. Diverse interpretations stand alongside each other, either as options or as conversation partners. Others understand postmodernism as a call for interpreters to assume greater ethical responsibility for what they say about the Bible. If there is no value-free interpretation, then the values one brings to interpretation must be named. Why do I interpret the way I do? Whose interests are being served? Whom does a particular interpretation oppress or liberate?

One example of this new attention to the ethical responsibility of biblical interpreters can be seen in how Christian discourse about Jews changed in the late twentieth century. As the horrors of the Holocaust became more apparent, Christian scholars struggled to understand not only Hitler as an individual but also the community mentality that made the extermination of Jews possible. While a range of factors has been named, many Christian theologians have acknowledged that the church's negative teachings about Jews helped lay the groundwork for genocide. In response, there has been a concerted effort in the past thirty years to counter Christian anti-Judaism. In a wide array of churches, the Jewishness of Jesus is stressed, and study guides for Holy Week now blame Jesus' death on selected Jewish leaders and/or the Roman Empire rather than the Jewish people as a whole. In many seminaries, "Old Testament" was renamed "Hebrew Bible" to avoid the suggestion that the first testament is outdated.

Sadly, greater commitment to Jews has made it difficult for many Christians to stand in solidarity with Palestinians. Palestinian Christian writers such as Naim Ateek and Mitri Raheb, along with Jewish writers such as Marc Ellis, have shown how the Holocaust has been used to deny land rights to Palestinians and to silence any criticism of the policies of the state of Israel. They have also shown the historical and ethical problems with assuming that God's promise of land to Abraham means that modern Israel belongs exclusively to Jews.

Where do you stand?

Few Christians today interpret the Bible in just one way. Most can identify elements of traditional, Enlightenment, and postmodern approaches to the Bible in themselves and in their churches. In my own teaching and preaching, I sometimes insist on particular criteria for "good" interpretation while in other cases I'm more open to a diversity of interpretation. I am well aware of many of the commitments and convictions that guide my use of diverse strategies, though regularly I am surprised by new insights into how and why I interpret the way I do.

The history of biblical interpretation underscores that what the Bible says (and what it means for the present) has never been simple or self-evident. No one reads the Bible "straight." Everyone interprets it. Even the self-proclaimed literalist makes certain assumptions about what the words on the page mean, how they apply to new situations, and which parts of the Bible carry the most importance.

That means that to use the Bible responsibly we have to do more than simply quote it. Bible verses don't settle debates, even though sometimes we try: "The Bible says it. I believe it. That settles it. (Now shut up.)" Responsible and fruitful discussion—about sexuality, social justice, end of life issues, etc.— demands the hard work of naming the values, assumptions, and beliefs that guide our moral decisions and that guide us to use the Bible the way we do.

Class Session

Spiritual Practice

As you begin your study, listen while the leader reads Acts 10:1-16. Following a few minutes of silence, consider what image, phrases or words "speak" to you today. Share your thoughts with the group.

Questions for Discussion:

1. Discuss the questions raised by the author in the introduction to this study:

> a) What relevance does the Bible have for contemporary life? Does the church still need this ancient docment?
> b) What about other arenas of life? Does the Bible be long in the court room, the science lab, the hospital ethics statement, and/or the bedroom?
> c) What does scripture say about science, for example, the creation of the earth and humankind, if anything? (You might choose to review Genesis 1:1-27.)
> d) Do you think the Bible is, in any way, a science book, or primarily a book of faith, spirituality, and ethical action?
> e) If the Bible is relevant to current cultural and ethical issues, how is it relevant? What principles should guide its application to the present?
> f) Are the words on the page self-evident? Or is biblical interpretation always more complicated than a simple reading might suggest?

2. Return to Acts 10:1-16. In this passage, God is apparently asking Peter to violate God's earlier laws, given to the children of Israel, about unclean food and unclean persons. What insights does this passage give about how some members of the early church viewed scripture?

3. Can you identify the different modes of interpretation presented by the author (ie., rule of faith, law of logic, diversity) and name times or places where you've found yourself applying them as the

guiding method of interpretation for your life? Where do you find yourself standing right now?

4. Realizing, with the author, that "there is no value-free interpretation" of the text and the need to name "the values one brings to interpretation," spend some time with the questions:

- Why do I interpret scripture the way I do? What past understandings and experiences guide my interpretation?
- Whose interests are being served?
- Whom does a particular interpretation oppress or liberate?

Conclude with a moment of prayer for insight in responding to the diverse interpretations in your congregation and among Christians.

NOTES:

SESSION FOUR

The Historical Critical Approach to Reading the Bible

Julia M. O'Brien

The method of biblical study known as Historical Criticism has both been praised as paving the way for interfaith understanding of the Bible and criticized as imposing narrow criteria for what the Bible can mean. Is either evaluation of this method fair? What is historical criticism, and what value does it have for the life of faith?

What is it?

In its most general sense, historical criticism refers to reading a text in its ancient context. What was going on in the world when a biblical passage was written and how does that information help us understand what it means?

Historical criticism often provides important background information for understanding a story. For example, the social structure of the ancient Israelite family helps explain why Esau and Jacob battle over birthright and blessing and what interest their mother Rebekah has in the outcome. Many readers of the story of David and Bathsheba want to know whether ancient women regularly bathed on roofs or why the death of Bathsheba's child is considered as punishment only for David. Inquiring biblical minds want to know lots of details: Who were the Samaritans, and why was it surprising for Jesus to cast one as the hero of his parable?   Why does the Old Testament never refer to cats or chickens?

The method, however, does more than offer background information. Historical criticism usually aspires for more, trying to reach behind a biblical account to determine when it was actually written. It refuses to assume that the time period a text talks <u>about</u> is the same time period in which it was <u>composed</u>. For example, the book of Joshua describes events that took place following the death of Moses and the book of Daniel sets its story in the Babylonian exile, but historians have argued that both were written hundreds of years later than the events they describe. These books, they claim, show us later authors retelling stories from the past in a particular way for a particular political and/or theological purpose.

The Origins of the Method

As described in the previous session, the logic behind historical criticism can be traced to the Enlightenment, when intellectuals in Europe and the New World began to apply the standard of Reason to all fields of human endeavor. Instrumental in applying this logic to the Bible was Baruch Spinoza, born in Amsterdam in 1632 to Jewish parents. Strongly influenced by the philosophers Rene Descartes and Thomas Hobbes, Spinoza argued that the Bible should be held to the same standards of reason that we apply to other literature and events. Since everything always happens according to natural law, we should attribute biblical events to natural rather than supernatural causes.

Nature is always the same, and its virtue and power of acting are everywhere one and the same. . . So the way of understanding the nature of anything, of whatever kind, must also be the same, viz. through the universal laws and rules of nature.

Spinoza's challenge to traditional Judaism led to his expulsion from the community, but his approach to the Bible grew in popularity after his death.

In the eighteenth and nineteenth centuries, European scholars developed historical criticism into an actual method and extended its influence. Perhaps the most famous example of their study regards the authorship of the Pentateuch, or the first five books of the Old Testament. Working carefully in the original languages, these scholars painstakingly detailed inconsistencies in these books: two creation accounts that differ in tone, order, and names of God; conflicting testimonies on how many animals entered Noah's ark; contrasting instructions about who may offer sacrifices; contrary guidance about the treatment of female slaves. These variations, argued scholars such as Jean Astruc and Wilhelm de Wette, challenge the traditional Jewish and Christian belief that Moses wrote the Pentateuch single-handedly. According to Julius Wellhausen's well-known Documentary Hypothesis, the Pentateuch is the combination of four originally-independent sources known as J, E, D, and P.

Historical critics also turned their attention to the New Testament. In the 1700's, Hermann Reimarus offered a natural explanation for Jesus' seemingly-miraculous feeding of the five thousand: the additional food appears not by supernatural intervention but Jesus' teaching opened the audience's heart to share the lunches they had brought from home. Historians of the New Testament also endeavored to explain the relationship between the gospels of Matthew, Mark, and Luke. If these gospels were written independently, why are they so similar? Why do some accounts of Jesus appear in all three gospels, other accounts in only Matthew and Luke, some only in Luke and some only in Matthew? By the late nineteenth century, the 2- Source Hypothesis was the reigning theory. It claims that Mark was written first and that Matthew and Luke used Mark as a source; that the additional material that Matthew and Luke share came from a source that has since been lost (named Q for "source"); and that Matthew and Luke additionally drew from a source unique to them. This theory is still popular today.

Even though, from its inception, historical criticism has faced opposition from some religious communities, by the beginning of the twentieth century, it had begun to find its way into the education of mainstream clergy. By the late 1940's, most main-line Protestant seminaries and divinity schools in Europe and the U.S. taught the historical critical method, training students of the Bible to ask about the intentions of its human authors. (Reminders of this legacy can be found at the back of the chapel at Lancaster Theological Seminary, where plaques honor the "Professor of Old Testament Science" and the "Professor of New Testament Science.")

In the mid-to-late twentieth century, various subdisciplines emerged within the field. Archaeologists attempted to find physical evidence of events and places described in the Bible. Sociologists studied other ancient and modern cultures for parallels that might explain Israelite group behavior. Form criticism analyzed the genre, or kinds, of biblical literature for clues to how the words had been passed down orally. Redaction critics focused on the work of biblical editors, those later hands that shaped ancient speeches and tales into their current form. While many of these interpreters stressed their differences from early historical critics, they shared the assumption that a text's meaning is rooted in what it meant in the past.

An Example of Historical Criticism: the Book of Jonah

How historical criticism works can be illustrated by applying it to the book of Jonah. Most Christians think of this story as a simple children's tale about a man who was swallowed by a whale. Some even confuse the story with another childhood story—that of Pinocchio, especially the Disney version; Gepetto and Jiminy Cricket find their way into the story, as does the assumption that the moral of this story is to tell the truth. When read through the lens of historical criticism, however, the book of Jonah is neither simple nor sweet.

Historians point to countless clues that the book is not a simple snapshot of exactly what happened in the past. It is riddled with historically-inaccurate details. According to the story, Jonah reluctantly travels to Nineveh, the capital of the kingdom of Assyria. He treks across the city, described as a three-days' walk across (2:3); he calls the people to repent, and the king of Nineveh and the entire population respond immediately. Historians point out various problems with this scenario. The city of Nineveh never had a king and, at its largest, extended three miles across and seven miles in circumference; a three-days' walk is usually calculated to 60 miles.

The city's size is not the only fantastic feature of this book. In chapter 1, pagan sailors immediately convert to the worship of Israel's God. In chapter 2, Jonah prays a beautifully-composed psalm while in the belly of a big fish, which spits him out after three days. In chapter 3, the entire city repents after Jonah proclaims a single sentence; even the animals fast and wear sackcloth. In chapter 4, a plant grows over Jonah's head in a single day and withers in a day, after being attacked by a worm. These are not everyday occurrences.

Moreover, the characters of Jonah do not act as the rest of the Bible would lead us to expect. Other prophetic books record what a figure proclaimed after accepting God's call to speak; this book records only one sentence of the prophet, devoting most of its time to relating the prophet's opposition to God's call and treatment of the Ninevites. Other prophetic books announce oracles against foreign nations in general and Assyria in particular, but in Jonah the sailors and the Assyrians respond far more quickly to God than the prophet himself. Especially ironic is the basis for Jonah's complaint in 4:2: he resents that God is gracious and merciful, the very characteristics of God most frequently praised in the Old Testament.

According to historical critics, all these clues suggest that the book of Jonah was artfully crafted as a satire. Its author did not intend readers to believe that Jonah was swallowed by a whale but instead to laugh at Jonah—and in turn to change their own "Jonah-like" behavior. Jonah resents God's extension of mercy to Israel's enemies; it makes him "angry enough to die" (4:9); the book itself shows how ridiculous Jonah's position is. The rhetorical question that closes the book is addressed not only to Jonah but also to the book's readers: if we care about our own unmerited comfort, should not God care about the ultimate fate of all people?

While historical critics debate the precise date of this book, its theme would have resonated sharply in the post-exilic period, when debates about the boundaries of the community were heated. The books of Nehemiah and Ezra report the decision to limit citizenship in the restored community to those Judeans who had returned from exile; Jonah, along with the book of Ruth, would have offered a challenge to such thinking.

Evaluating Historical Criticism

In insisting that the meaning of the Bible is determined by critical analysis rather than one's religious or political beliefs, historical criticism has made it possible for people with different beliefs to discuss the Bible with one another. Jews and Christians might not agree about Jesus' role in the divine plan of salvation but they might be able to reach consensus on who wrote the book of Isaiah and why. Roman Catholics might include more books in their canon than Protestants do, but both can evaluate clues to the author of the book of Tobit. Indeed, historical study can be undertaken by those who claim no religious faith, allowing biblical studies to operate as a respectable academic discipline in secular universities.

Many see this development as a welcome respite from religious bickering and as opening biblical study to a wider audience. But the distance that historical criticism creates between study and belief also has generated harsh criticism. Within academic circles, postmodern interpreters have protested that this method fails to recognize its own interests and biases. Feminist scholars have argued that what has passed as objective study has often been guided by patriarchal, or male-oriented, assumptions, and interpreters in non-Western cultures have shown how the Western definition of reason casts the wisdom of their own societies as superstitious or irrelevant to serious study.

Many Christians also have protested that historical criticism ignores the wisdom of the church as well as the spiritual aspects of Scripture. Some seminaries and divinity schools are shifting the focus of biblical study away from the ancient world to what the church has taught about the Bible and to what the contemporary community hears in its witness. The Bible is taught in its "canonical context" rather than its ancient context: rather than attempt to reconstruct what texts meant to their authors and original communities, students are taught to interpret the Bible as it has come to us through generations of the faithful. To read theologically, one must start with the core confessions of the church.

Although historical criticism's hold on Christian interpretation today is less strong than in the mid-twentieth century, even most postmodern interpreters still recognize the ancient context of the Bible as one important layer of its meaning. Academics continue to study and parishioners continue to ask what Moses and Jesus were really like, whether the walls of Jericho really fell at the blast of a trumpet, and whether the books of Daniel and Revelation were intended to predict our future. The question for Christians is not whether historical study has <u>any</u> merit but rather <u>how much</u>: how much weight should our reconstructions of the past lend to our understanding and to the meaning (s) of Scripture?

Class Session

Spiritual Practice

Begin today's class with a time of silence, during which the leader reads Jonah 3:3b-4:4. Following the reading of the passage, take a few minutes to reflect in silence on the word, phrase, or image that "speaks" to you today. After a few minutes of silence, share as a group what words or images spoke to you.

Questions for Discussion:

1. Our author points out: "The rhetorical question that closes the book is addressed not only to Jonah but also to the book's readers: if we care about our own unmerited comfort, should not God care about the ultimate fate of all people?" Discuss this statement within the group and share your insights. Do we struggle with boundary debates today in our society? What do you believe our faith says to us within our own debates?

2. Why might the historical critical approach be helpful to use when studying biblical texts? Does this method challenge your previous understandings of how to read sacred texts? If so, in what ways?

3. Are there particular bible "stories" that you think might be opened to greater understanding and deeper meaning as historical criticism is applied to them?

4. Were there new insights or surprises for you in the historical critical look at the Book of Jonah?

5. Do you think it's important for people with different beliefs to have a method whereby they can approach Biblical texts together? Why or why not? What about those with no religious belief, is it valuable/desirable that the texts are accessible to those whose approach may be secular in nature?

6. The author asks us to consider the question of how much merit historical criticism has for us as we approach our sacred text. How would you answer her question?

Conclude the session by reading Jonah 4:9-11 and consider prayerfully the "strangers" or "outsiders" toward which God may be calling us to reach out.

NOTES:

SESSION FIVE

A Literary Approach To The Bible
Greg Carey

Read John 3:1-21 and 4:4-42.

The historical critical approach transformed biblical interpretation. No longer could church authorities tell people what the Bible could – and couldn't – mean. Interpreters like Martin Luther and John Calvin insisted that it mattered when, where, and why the biblical authors wrote. They also insisted on the power for every person to ask such questions and arrive at their own answers. Historical approaches to the Bible represented a necessary condition for the Protestant Reformation.

However, historical interpretation also represented a loss for readers of the Bible – or more properly, several losses. Before we reflect on literary approaches, we might count the cost of a strictly historical approach.

First, biblical truth gradually came to be equated with historical accuracy. For many people, the value of a biblical story roughly amounts to whether the events it describes actually happened. That's a shame. This way of thinking leads Christians to build things like Kentucky's Creation Museum, where vegetarian dinosaurs live side by side with Eve and Adam. Unfortunately, when we reduce biblical truth to events in the past, we lose the ability to ask the most important questions: What does Genesis 1 say about humanity's role in creation? What does Genesis 2-3 (the Adam & Eve story) teach us about human nature? What important questions and insights emerge when we compare the two stories of creation (Genesis 1:1-2:4a and Genesis 2:4b-3:24)? We might recall Jesus' parables: when Jesus wanted to communicate something important, he often made up a story. A narrow interest in history closes off the major questions of faith, the very questions that motivated the biblical authors.

Second, our focus zoomed in from the biblical story, and stories as a whole, to ever smaller bits of biblical data. To change metaphors, historically oriented interpreters apply archaeological tools, picking and digging through the biblical stories to find the historical layers underneath. We've learned a great deal from this work. We can assess – often with some confidence – the processes of oral tradition, literary production, and editing that led to the formation of important parts of the Bible. However, the effect of such work takes our eyes away from the big picture. Why does Genesis have two stories in which Abraham goes into a foreign land and passes off Sarah as his sister? From an historical point of view, it's because the authors of Genesis (clumsily) combined parallel stories. But from a literary point of view we look at the whole story: it's one thing for Abraham to throw Sarah to the wolves once, quite another thing to watch him do it twice.

A third result of a narrow historical approach was inevitable. People lost the ability to recognize the artistry of the biblical stories (and other kinds of literature, even Paul's letters). In the New Testament, the author of Mark used to be accused of a rough, rustic, or unsophisticated style. Mark's Greek isn't particularly fancy, and the Gospel has a way of connecting stories with the phrase, "And immediately." (Immediately shows up 43 times in Mark.) But "uneducated" does not equal "unsophisticated" or "dull." Many popular storytellers use highly sophisticated techniques. In the 1980s and 90s, interpreters began to notice that Mark displays a wide variety of literary tricks. If Mark wants to emphasize a point, we'll find key phrases or scenes repeated. Mark almost never quotes the Hebrew Scriptures, but Mark evokes particular passages by setting up the scene. When Jesus feeds a crowd of 5,000 (that's just the men), he notices that they are "like sheep without a shepherd" (6:34). He has the crowd lie down on the green grass (notice how rarely color figures in biblical stories), and he takes, blesses, breaks, and gives the loaves to the crowd (Mark uses the same verbs, in the same order, at the Last Supper). Sheep needing a shepherd, green grass, a distributed meal. . . "The LORD is my shepherd. . . He makes me to lie down in green pastures. . . He prepares a table before me. . ." What is Mark saying about Jesus here?

What **Is** a Literary Approach?

How does a literary approach to the Bible work? Basically, literary interpretation means that we attend to the Bible's artfulness. We notice how biblical storytellers place their stories in significant times, places, and social settings. When a biblical story changes pace, we discern a change in mood. We pay attention not just to what we learn about David or the disciples but how we learn these things. Does the storyteller inform us? Do we learn from other characters? Is it up to us to decide who a character is on the basis of her speech and actions? We delight in the Bible's propensity to build comparisons and contrasts, to repeat certain words or motifs, to sandwich one story within another, to draw the focus to a particular character or event. We get the point when one biblical story draws its inspiration from another. We especially relish how biblical stories can build suspense before they reach their apex – or sometimes, before they frustrate us by heading off in a new direction.

Before we consider some examples, I'll suggest another benefit from literary approaches. Why do we read literature? Basically, there are two reasons: literature is both rewarding and fun. Many times a story or a film has led me to look at life in a fresh way. That's not so far from what we expect from the Bible. But those rewards come with entertainment – and many of the Bible's stories entertain even as they instruct us.

An Example: David's Turning Point

Popular imagination holds David as a gifted, but tragically flawed spiritual genius. The David whose faith empowered him to defeat Goliath, and whose vibrant spirit is commemorated by the many Psalms attributed to him is also the David who took Bathsheba and murdered her husband Uriah. We hear less often how David's misconduct represents a dramatic turning point in his career. His repentance does not save him from misfortune. For the rest of David's life, and even beyond his life, violence hounds the king and his household.

We encounter this turning point in 2 Samuel 11-12. The prophet Nathan confronts David concerning his sin and the judgment he faces.

Now the LORD has put away your sin; you shall not die. Nevertheless, because by this deed you have utterly scorned the LORD, the child that is born to you shall die. (12:13-14)

Let's pay attention to David's reaction, particularly to how the story reveals David's character through his reaction. (Please look up 2 Samuel 12:15-25.)

- First, when the child falls ill David responds just as we'd predict. He goes into a severe discipline of fasting and prayer. We learn this because the narrator of the story tells us so.
- Second, David's servants reveal more about his character. When the child dies, they're afraid to tell the king: he might hurt himself. We learn about David by what other characters say.
- Third, David perceives that the child has died from the behavior of his servants. Again, the narrator tells us this, but we also see it through David's behavior and speech.
- Once the child has died, David rises, goes to worship the LORD, and eats. Now his servants are confused: "Why did you fast when the child was sick, but now that the child is dead you eat?" The servants' speech raises suspense concerning the kind of person David is.
- Finally, David explains his behavior. "What's the

point in fasting and weeping now that the child is dead? Will I bring him back to life?" Here David speaks for himself.

David then consoles Bathsheba, sleeping with her again so that she conceives another son, Solomon.

So far, the story has informed us about David through several literary techniques. There's what the narrator tells us about David, how David behaves, what other characters say about him, and what David says about himself. But there's one more thing: What do you think about David's reaction to the child's death? The story has given us several clues concerning David, but it also raises several questions. (1) Is David a man of courage and faith, who accepts the child's death with equanimity? (2) Is David so cold blooded that the child's death does not affect him? (3) Is David's fasting and prayer an act of genuine spirituality, or is it a sham designed to manipulate God?

Beyond the Stories

Literary approaches are most at home with stories and poems, but we may apply them to other forms of literature as well. For example, if you browse Paul's First letter to the Thessalonians, you'll notice how the tone and pace change right at the end of chapter 3. It's a short letter, only five chapters long, and yet the first three chapters all look back to the past. It's almost like a love song with, "Remember how we first met," as the chorus. For three of the five chapters, Paul continues to celebrate his relationship with the Thessalonians and their faithfulness.

Only in chapter four does Paul begin dealing out advice. Be careful about sex (8 verses; 4:1-8). Keep on loving one another (4 verses; 4:9-12). But these bits of exhortation pass by quickly; it's as if Paul just wants them out of the way. But things slow way down at 4:13 because Paul must address a tricky subject: what about believers who die before the Lord's return? Notice how the pace changes; how Paul introduces rich, vivid imagery; how he develops his arguments more fully. The discussion about death and Jesus' return takes 17 verses; after it, Paul begins to bring the letter to a close.

If we pay attention to the letter's pacing, how much time it spends on certain topics, we notice a pattern.

- The first three chapters are very slow, almost entirely related to things that have happened in the past.
- Then we cover two topics quickly, sex (4:1-8) and community (4:9-12).
- Just before the close of the letter, we slow down again and discuss a single topic at length, the problem of death, resurrection, and Jesus' return (4:13-5:11).
- Finally, the letter rushes to its conclusion with a series of exhortations.

Based on pacing, many interpreters believe the problem of Jesus' return is the main reason Paul wrote 1 Thessalonians. It must have been a sensitive subject, given how carefully Paul sets up the conversation. Paul takes time to build up his relationship with the Thessalonians, he breezes through a couple of topics, and he slows down again for the touchy subject.

A Story with Suspense

Literary approaches can help us appreciate how biblical stories move in time. Because we're already familiar with many biblical stories, we forget what it would be like to hear them for the first time. If we don't know how the story will turn out, we have the ability to experience suspense and surprise.

We don't often think of it this way, but the book of Revelation is a story. It relates a vision that happened to an ancient Christian prophet named John. And the story has suspense. Let's look at one unfamiliar passage, Revelation 5:1-13.

John has ascended into heaven, where "the one seated upon the throne" – that's God in apocalyptic literature – holds a sealed scroll. As we'll soon find out, the scroll will relate the unfolding of human history; its contents pretty much amount to the rest of the book of Revelation. John "weeps bitterly" because no one is able – or worthy – to unseal the scroll. This is suspense.

Then one of the heavenly elders speaks up: the Lion of Judah has conquered, qualifying him to open the seals. Good news! A fierce lion to take up the cause! Up to this point Revelation has been all about conquest, enduring the forces of evil despite the churches' evident weakness, despite persecution. What these vulnerable little communities of Jesus' followers need is a lion. The Lion is worthy....

So John looks for the Lion, and you know what? The Lion never shows up. No Lion ever appears in Revelation. In the Lion's place stands a Lamb "standing as if it had been slaughtered," The Lamb is worthy to unseal the scrolls because through its death it has redeemed a people. Through its faithful witness (1:5), the Lamb has demonstrated its worth.

Throughout the rest of Revelation, we'll see the Lamb; No Lion, but the Lamb. The point? In the face of overwhelming imperial pressure ("Who is like the Beast, and who can fight against it?" 13:4), in the face of ostracism and persecution, God rules not by Lion Power but by Lamb Power. Faithful witness, endurance, boundless love. Those win the day. Lamb Power, not Lion Power. Revelation accomplishes this effect through suspense and surprise.

Class Session

Spiritual Practice

Begin class with a time of silence, during which the leader reads John 3:1-21 and 4:4-42. Following the reading of the passages, take time in silence to reflect on what word, image or phrase "speaks" to you today. After a few minutes of silence, share your reflections with the group.

Questions for discussion:

1. Invite class members to reflect on the introductory essay.

    a) Having studied historical approaches to the Bible last week, how do they feel about literary approaches?

        i. Does anything about literary approaches make you feel uncomfortable?

        ii. Do literary approaches help you see new things in biblical stories and other literature?

        iii. In your opinion, can a story reveal the truth without involving something that actually happened just as it's described?

    b) In how many ways does 2 Samuel 12:15-25 provide information about David?

2. Allow class members time to re-scan John 3:1-21 and 4:4-42. Begin with the question: Do the stories of Nicodemus and the Samaritan Woman have anything in common? What differences do you observe?

    a) Readers may note that both stories involve a meandering series of questions and answers. Both stories also have Jesus speaking in metaphorical ways that confuse his conversation partners. Is it born again, or born from above? What is that living water? May I have a drink?

    b) Readers may also note that while Nicodemus never seems to get it, the Samaritan Woman becomes an effective evangelist.

3. Compare the settings for Jesus' encounters with Nicodemus

and the Samaritan woman.

    a) Where do they meet?

    b) When do they meet?

    c) Observe: Many interpreters have suggested that Jesus meets the woman at noon because of her personal life. According to this line of thought, most people visited wells in the cool of the morning, not in the noontime heat. Perhaps the woman avoids public attention by coming when the well will be abandoned.

    d) Invite the class to re-read John 3:17-21. What does the Gospel say about light and dark? In light of these verses, do you find it significant that Nicodemus comes at night while the Samaritan woman comes at noon?

4. Invite the class to ponder these two conversations.

    a) Both Nicodemus and the Samaritan woman misunder-stand Jesus at certain points.
    What, do you think, is the cause of their confusion? Are they dull, or is Jesus difficult to understand? Why do you think so?

    b) Eventually, the Samaritan woman becomes an effec tive witness for Jesus in her village. Nicodemus, how-ever, continues to follow Jesus – but only at night (John 7:45-52; 19:38-42). Why do you think the Sa-maritan woman comes to believe in Jesus, while Nico-demus remains confused at the end of our story?

Conclude by prayerfully asking God to give us "more light" on the scriptures, so that we might know its meaning for us in our time and place.

NOTES:

SESSION SIX

The Voices of the Prophets
Julia M. O'Brien

Who's a Prophet?

Was Rev. Martin Luther King, Jr. a prophet? How about Mother Teresa? Nostradamus? Leonardo da Vinci? Hildegard of Bingen? Billy Graham? Rachel Carson? Bob Marley? Marian Wright Edelman? Tim LaHaye? Your grandmother?

Obviously, your answers depend on your definition of a prophet. Is a prophet someone through whom God relays privileged information? Does a prophet predict what will happen in the future? Are prophets faith-based social analysts who explain current events in terms of divine will? Are they critics of unjust social policies? Does a prophet spit slam poetry to shock us with the truth? Are prophets preachers who call us back to God? Are they moral guides, teachers of proper behavior?

Common Definitions

Prophets have been described in all these ways—and others. But perhaps the most enduring definition of a prophet is as someone who predicts the future, who knows ahead of time what will happen. Many parts of the Bible lend support to such an understanding. Deuteronomy 18:22 lists accuracy of prediction as the first criterion for identifying true prophecy: "When a prophet speaks in the name of the LORD, if the thing does not come about or come true, that is the thing which the LORD has not spoken."

In the same way, 1 and 2 Kings go to great lengths to show that events conform to prophetic predictions: in 2 Kings 9, the Israelite queen Jezebel was killed in the exact way the prophet Elisha had foretold. Many New Testament writers also treat the words of the prophets as predictions: the first two chapters of the gospel of Matthew cite five Old Testament prophecies fulfilled by Jesus' birth. This approach to prophecy is familiar to most of us, especially those who sing the Advent hymn "Lo, How a Rose," listen to Handel's Messiah, or gaze at paintings in which Isaiah hovers above or below the infant Jesus and his mother.

"Prophetic" has taken on a different meaning in socially progressive churches, where it refers to speaking courageously against injustice. Assuming a "prophetic" role in the pulpit or the public square means to confront oppressive individuals and institutions, to speak truth to power. Support for this definition of prophecy can also be found in the Bible, especially in the "classical prophets"—books devoted to the words and actions of a single prophet. The books of Amos, Micah, and Jeremiah portray these prophets as standing against adversaries to speak God's truth. They risk popularity and physical safety to insist on God's demand to "do justice, love goodness and walk modestly with your God" (Micah 6:8). Because these same prophets often critique religious ritual, progressives also turn to their words to support their own conviction that God cares more about how we treat others than how we conduct worship services. In this line of interpretation, Jesus becomes the ultimate prophetic figure: even death could not stop his courageous challenge to oppressive religious and political policies.

Whose Voice do we Hear in Prophetic Books?

Both of these understandings of prophets--as foretellers and as social activists--find support in the Bible and in popular imagination. But careful study highlights aspects of the prophetic books that caution us from being too confident that we know exactly who prophets were and what they did.

First, readers should recognize how little we know about

the "historical" prophets. Apart from basic information given in introductory statements (called superscriptions), the prophetic books give us few biographical details about the prophets. Were they educated? Did they worship in the Temple? Who were their parents or their siblings? How old were they? Where did they proclaim their speeches?

Little information is available to supplement the information that the prophetic books themselves provide: most are not mentioned elsewhere in the Bible, and no documents outside the Bible mention them.

Moreover, numerous features of the books indicate that they were written not by the prophets themselves but by others. The superscriptions are words about the prophet rather than by him, and accounts of the prophet's actions are usually written in third person: "here is what the prophet did and said."

Several centuries of scholarship on the prophetic books have highlighted how complex these books really are and how carefully they have been composed. The books of Isaiah, Micah and Zechariah, for example, are likely the blending of originally-separate writings with diverse perspectives. The ending of Habakkuk and the beginning of Nahum seem to have incorporated psalms, and the announcement that "the LORD roars from Zion" both ends Joel and begins Amos (which follows it). The book of Jeremiah looks so different in the Hebrew text (on which the NRSV is based) than in the ancient Greek translation known as the Septuagint that some scholars think two different versions of the book must have circulated for a long time. Clearly, these books are not first-hand transcripts of prophetic speeches but instead artful compositions written by later communities.

For these reasons as well as others, contemporary scholars insist that we ask fewer questions about the personalities of individual prophets and more about why communities of faith created the books that they did. What did they want readers to remember about the prophets? Why did they think those memories were important? What impression did they want to create? What insights did they want to convey? What reactions were they trying to provoke?

This shift of focus from prophets to prophetic books has implications for the church. It calls us away from lauding prophets as Lone Rangers, solitary voices crying in the wilderness, and calls us to paying greater attention to the communal aspects of prophecy. If a prophetic book is the witness of communities over time, then it should invite us to look for the wisdom of those communities as well as for the wisdom of our own communities of faith.

This shift of locus also suggests that we think of prophecy less as prediction and more as interpretation of the past. If the accounts were written after the fact, they show communities trying to understand their past for the sake of their present. How did they see God working in the past? What does that suggest about how they thought God might be working in their own day? What did they think readers can learn from the past that might prove helpful for moving forward?

The Voice(s) of the Interpreter

In the past fifty years, professional biblical scholarship has undergone significant demographic changes. Women, Asian- and African-Americans, LGBT folks, and persons from the Two-Thirds World have joined their white male counterparts in giving papers at professional conferences, publishing biblical commentaries, and generally making their voices heard.

These "new" voices have insisted that prophetic speech sometimes contributes to (rather than challenges) injustice. The most frequently-cited example is the attention that feminist interpreters have drawn to the prophetic "marriage metaphor," the comparison of God's relationship to Israel/Judah to that between a husband and wife. The metaphor, which appears not only in Hosea but throughout the prophetic books, describes marriage as an unequal partnership: the husband chooses the wife, can send away his wife, and has the right to punish the wife (physically) for any infidelity. The sins and the looming punishment of the unfaithful woman are frequently described in graphic, sexualized terms: Ezekiel 23 not only details Israel and Judah's sexual proclivities but also announces that, as adulterers, they will be stoned to death. In the book of Nahum, the city of Nineveh is cast as a prostitute whom God the Warrior will sexually humiliate.

Feminists have argued that these images negatively affect people in the present. The marriage metaphor gives divine sanction to male control of women and reinforces the logic that drives domestic violence. They call readers to recognize the danger of prophetic speech alongside gifts to the church. The prophets are not ethical models to be imitated; rather, these books confront us with powerful words that we must find a way to use responsibly.

Even though today most interpreters recognize the sexism of prophetic speech, earlier generations of interpreters did not. To see these and other previously-ignored aspects of the text, new interpretative lenses are needed. As the church interprets the prophets, then, it needs to pay attention not only to who is speaking in a prophetic book but also who is speaking about the book. Whose voices are we missing? We need to hear interpreters different from ourselves to notice our blind spots and avoid unwittingly reinforcing harmful attitudes.

The Case of Amos

The book of Amos provides a good testing ground for the different understandings of the prophets that I've discussed.

Prediction or Interpretation?

Amos is presented as predicting the fall of the nation of Israel before it took place. Throughout the book, the prophet insists that Israel and its capital Samaria face impending doom. In 4:1-4, the women of Samaria are threatened with destruction, and in 5:16-17 all Israel is told to prepare for punishment to come. Chapter 9 contains the direst prediction: for its sin, God will destroy the nation of Israel. Since the book's opening superscription dates Amos to around 750 BCE and since the nation of Israel did fall to the Assyrian armies thirty years later, Amos is described as accurately foretelling the nation's destruction.

Several clues in the book, however, suggest that the book itself was written after the fall of Samaria in 722/721. The superscription, for example, seems to have been written in retrospect. Also, perspectives other than those of the historical Amos seem to have been included. This is seen most pointedly in the book's happy ending. Amos 9:11-15 provides not only the book's only note of hope but also its only mention of David. It predicts the restoration of the royal line of David, indicating that at the time of writing there was no Davidic king; it also refers to a time when only a remnant of the nation of Edom remains. These descriptions do not fit the eighth century, when Amos lived, but rather the fifth century—usually called the Persian or postexilic period.

If composed during the Persian period, the book of Amos would have served to explain to a later generation why the nation of Israel once fell and caution its readers not to make the same mistakes. The book of Zechariah, which was written in the Persian period, understands the earlier prophets in exactly this way:

> "Return to me," declares the LORD Almighty, "and I will return to you," says the LORD Almighty. Do not be like your forefathers, to whom the earlier prophets proclaimed: This is what the LORD Almighty says: "Turn from your evil ways and your evil practices." But they would not listen or pay attention to me, declares the LORD. Where are your forefathers now? And the prophets, do they live forever? But did not my words and my decrees, which I commanded my servants the prophets, overtake your forefathers? (Zechariah 1:3-6)

Social Justice for Everybody?

Amos lobs its most stinging critiques against those who oppress the poor. In bold hyperbole, it describes the wealthy as "selling the righteous for silver" (2:6), and in humiliating caricature it depicts the wealthy women of Samaria as "cows of Bashan" (4:1). The nation fell, according to Amos, not because of sexual immorality, poor military strategy, or corrupt leaders, but because its citizens did not care for their neighbors.

Understandably, this focus has made Amos a favorite of those who place economic and social justice at the heart of religious faith. Many have joined Martin Luther King, Jr. in making Amos' cry for justice their own: "let justice roll down like waters and righteousness like an everflowing stream" (5:24). Liberation theologians, who argue that faithful Christians should be concerned not primarily with life after death but more importantly with the real conditions in which people live now, find in Amos a kindred spirit.

At least one scholar, however, has shown how Amos falls short of all-inclusive justice. In the Women's Bible Commentary (Westminster John Knox, 1992), Judith Sanderson claims that the description of Samarian women in 4:1-3 unfairly scapegoats women for the nation's ills. Since in all cultures women make up a disproportionate percentage of the poor, she laments that "Amos specifically condemned wealthy women for oppressing the poor (4:1) but failed specifically to champion the women among the poor" (p. 206). If in ancient Israel women neither owned nor controlled property, why do they bear sole responsibility for how their husbands disseminate wealth?

Amos is certainly not unique in falling short of a truly inclusive vision of justice, and we need not dismiss the book because of its blind spots. But it is important to recognize that Amos—and the rest of the prophets--may not offer the last word on what God's full justice might entail.

Conclusions

This session has stressed that the prophets are more complex than simple definitions might suggest. Through the prophetic books, ancient communities speak to us of their memories and their values, some of which inspire us and others which trouble us. Reading these books carefully requires that we listen respectfully to what they have to say but also that we speak out when their portraits of God and our neighbors do either a disservice.

Class Study

Spiritual Practice

As you prepare to study together, listen as the leader reads Amos 5:18-24. After a few minutes of silence share with one another any words, images or phrases that "spoke" to you today.

Questions for discussion:

1. How do <u>you</u> define or think about the name "prophet?" Where do you hear the word used in popular media or religion?

2. Our author tells us that contemporary scholars ask us to focus less on "the prophet" and more on understanding why faith communities created the books they did, and that this shift in focus has implications for the church. Explore some of the questions raised by the author:

- How did the communities see God working in the past?

- What does that suggest about how God was at work in their own time?

- What did they think folk might learn from the past that would help them as they move forward in the future?

- How are <u>we</u> today impacted by this understanding of "the voices of the prophets?"

3. Was there anything new or surprising in the glimpse of Amos presented in the study? How was your idea of social justice deepened or stretched?

4. Do you think the prophet's concern for social justice applies to us today? What might "let justice roll down like waters and righteousness like an ever-flowing stream" mean to us today?

5. Walter Brueggemann speaks of the prophetic imagination as the presentation of an "alternative reality" to the present state of affairs. From the prophetic perspective, what areas of our social life might be judged in light of an alternative understanding of God's will? Where do we fall short of embodying God's king-

dom, or realm, "on earth as it is in heaven?"

6. React to the statement: "it is important to recognize that Amos – and the rest of the prophets – may not offer the last word on what God's full justice might entail."

What problems does the author notice in Amos? Are today's justice seekers also capable of omitting the well-being of or unfairly caricaturing certain members of our society?

Conclude by lifting up neglected people in our society. Ask for guidance in terms of how you or your church might creatively respond to their needs.

NOTES:

SESSION SEVEN

The Voices Of The Gospels

Greg Carey

Read chapters 1, 2, and 28 of Matthew , chapters 1 and 16 of Mark, chapters 1, 2, and 24 of Luke, and chapters 1, 20, and 21 of John, mindful of how each Gospel tells its story differently.

The Book of Kells, that richly illuminated Celtic copy of the Gospels, includes a representation of the four Gospels: Matthew as a human being; Mark as a lion; Luke as an ox; and John as an eagle. These symbols have represented the four Gospels since at least the second century. Today we can find them in Protestant and Catholic churches all over our cities and counties.

Throughout the centuries, these symbols have functioned to remind Christians that each Gospel has its own distinctive voice. Matthew's presentation of Jesus complements that of Luke, but they are not exactly the same. Back when very few Christians could read the Gospels for themselves, the four symbols performed an important teaching function. Jesus was born, really and truly, as a human (Matthew). He reigns like a lion (Mark). Like an ox, Jesus carried the burdens of humanity, as he calls his disciples to do (Luke). And his origins and destiny reside in the heavens, like an eagle (John). Each of these symbols embodies the particular qualities of its respective Gospel.

Richard A. Burridge's short introduction to the *Gospels, Four Gospels, One Jesus?* (Grand Rapids: Eerdmans, 1994) begins with an introduction to these symbols.

Some Christians find the Gospels' diversity surprising, even troubling. If you go to a Christian bookstore, you can quickly find a "Harmony of the Gospels." Some study Bibles even include one. A Harmony of the Gospels takes the four Gospels, and then combines them into one single, consistent narrative. That's pretty hard to do. For example, did Jesus drive the moneychangers out of the temple once or twice? All of the Gospels tell the story once, but John places it near the beginning of Jesus' ministry. How many times did a woman come to anoint Jesus? Again, one such story for each Gospel, but Luke's comes much earlier in the story and the details are quite different. Nevertheless, consistency is so important to some Christians that they'll go to just about any length to harmonize the stories.

However, Christians have long known that each Gospel offers its own contribution. The first attempt to harmonize the Gospels happened back in the second century. A Christian named Tatian composed the Diatessaron, which achieved wide popularity. (Diatessaron means, "through four.") Over time, Tatian's contribution declined in influence – rapidly in some parts of the church, but less so in others. Likewise, some ancient copyists of the Gospels edited their manuscripts so as to remove any perceived contradictions. But again, most copyists preferred to leave things as they were, valuing diversity over agreement.

While the Diatessaron was circulating around the Mediterranean world, Christian leaders were insisting on the value of four Gospels – not just one. Irenaeus, bishop of Lyons, maintained that the four Gospels were absolutely necessary. We might not find this argument persuasive, but some ancient people apparently did:

> The Gospels could not possibly be either more or less in number than they are. Since there are four zones of the

world in which we live, and four principal winds, while the Church is spread over all the earth, and the pillar and foundation of the Church is the gospel, and the Spirit of life, it fittingly has four pillars, everywhere breathing out incorruption and revivifying men. From this it is clear that the Word, the artificer of all things, being manifested to men gave us the gospel, <u>fourfold in form but held together by one Spirit</u>. (Against Heresies 3.11.8)

Four "zones of the world," four directions of the wind, and four Gospels. Right? If we get stuck on Irenaeus' peculiar logic, we'll miss the main point. Irenaeus finds it essential that we possess four diverse Gospels, but they all participate in one larger truth.

The Value of Diversity

When I teach introductory courses on the Gospels, I have two primary goals. One is for students to develop their skills at biblical interpretation. The second is for students to appreciate the distinctive voice of each of the Gospels. We assess this learning by giving quizzes. Students take their first quiz on the very first day of class. It includes quotes from the Gospels, and they're supposed to recognize the source Gospel for each quote. Pretty hard, huh? The average grade on that quiz – don't worry, it doesn't count – is just over 30 percent. By the end of the semester we give a very similar quiz, and students typically score over 80 percent. In other words, once you're really familiar with the Gospels, you can recognize each one's unique characteristics.

One can easily overstate the differences among the Gospels. All four Gospels have Jesus gathering disciples, healing people, participating in communal meals, engaging in conflict with the religious authorities of his day, enduring crucifixion after a double trial, and rising from the dead. All four depict Jesus as the messiah of Israel, come to bring salvation to humankind.

Just the same, the Gospels all have their distinctive concerns, sometimes in conflict with one another. Let's take one example. Almost all biblical scholars agree that whoever wrote the

Gospels of Matthew and Luke possessed a copy of Mark and used it as a source. Most of the time, Matthew (especially) and Luke share the same stories we find in Mark, in the same order, and with many of the same Greek words.

One of Mark's characteristics is that Jesus' humanity comes through so strongly. For example, when Jesus teaches in Nazareth, his hometown, things don't go well. The townsfolk don't believe, and "he could do no deed of power there, except that he laid his hands on a few sick people and cured them" (Mark 6:5). Matthew tells the same story, but with a significant twist: "he did not do many deeds of power there, because of their unbelief" (13:58). (Luke tells the story very differently in 4:16-30).

Likewise, Mark describes the woman with the hemorrhage who is healed when she touches Jesus' cloak. Let's compare Matthew and Mark (again, Luke 8:43-48 has a slightly different version).

Matthew 9:22	Mark 5:29-32
NRS Matthew 9:22 Jesus turned, and seeing her he said, "Take heart, daughter; your faith has made you well." And instantly the woman was made well.	NRS Mark 5:29 Immediately her hemorrhage stopped; and she felt in her body that she was healed of her disease. 30 Immediately aware that power had gone forth from him, Jesus turned about in the crowd and said, "Who touched my clothes?" 31 And his disciples said to him, "You see the crowd pressing in on you; how can you say, 'Who touched me?'" 32 He looked all around to see who had done it.

75

Notice two significant differences between Matthew's version and Mark's. (1) Mark's Jesus does not know who touched him, nor do his disciples. Jesus "looked all around" to see who had touched him. But Matthew's Jesus does not struggle with human limitations in the same way that Mark's Jesus does. In Matthew Jesus turns, sees the woman, and speaks to her. (2) In Mark the woman is healed immediately upon touching Jesus, but Matthew emphasizes Jesus' power by delaying her healing until Jesus speaks to her.

Here we have two slightly different understandings of Jesus and his healing power. Both Matthew and Mark agree that Jesus heals people miraculously. Mark's Jesus does so because the power of God is working in him, even beyond his own control, while Matthew's Jesus possesses divine insight.

Each Gospel in Its Own Voice

Besides comparing specific passages, another way to compare the Gospels is to look at their beginnings and endings. Sure enough, the opening and closing of each Gospel reflects some of its crucial characteristics.

A British scholar named Morna Hooker has done just that in a couple of books, *Beginnings: Keys That Open the Gospels* (Harrisburg: Trinity Press International, 1997), and *Endings: Invitations to Discipleship* (London: SCM, 2003).

Matthew

Matthew begins with the famous genealogy: Jesus the Messiah, son of David, son of Abraham. Most genealogies are boring, but this one fascinates for several reasons. (Why not look up the stories of the four women included in the genealogy?) In Matthew's case, the story of Jesus is a continuation of the story of Israel. Luke describes Jesus as "son of Adam," indicating his relationship to all people, but Matthew emphasizes Jesus' Jewishness.

The genealogy rehearses the high points of Israel's story. It begins with Abraham, the "father" of the nation. After fourteen names, it moves to David, Israel's great king. Indeed, in chapter 2 the king, Herod, is terrified that Jesus' birth threatens his own throne. Fourteen more names and we arrive at a definitive moment in Israel's history, the exile to Babylon. Fourteen more names and we arrive at Jesus. Jesus is the continuation of all that God has been doing from Abraham through David, even through the exile.

Jesus' childhood and early ministry correspond to the story of Israel's exodus from Egypt in several ways.

- Both stories depict a great tyrant who slaughters innocent male children.
- Both stories include foreign astrologers.
- Both stories involve time spent in Egypt.
- Both stories involve the Jordan River.
- And, in chapter 3, Jesus goes into the desert for forty days and nights, fed by God, just as Israel wandered in the desert for forty years, fed by God.

All of these parallels remind us of the story of Moses and Israel. Just as Moses delivers the Law from Mount Sinai, Jesus goes up on a mountain to interpret the Law for his disciples in the Sermon on the Mount (Matthew 5-7).

Matthew presents Jesus as an authoritative teacher of the Law. Most interpreters believe that this Gospel was written for Jewish Christians who continued to observe the Law even as they followed Jesus. Matthew's Jesus expects his disciples to do everything he teaches them (7:21-29). Indeed, he tells them:

Don't even think that I've come to abolish the law and the prophets. I have come not to abolish them but to fulfill. For truly I tell you, until heaven and earth pass away, not one letter, not one stroke of a letter, will pass from the law until all is accomplished. (5:17-18, author's translation)

It's no wonder, then, that the last instructions from the

risen Jesus to his disciples include this saying:

> Go therefore and make disciples of all nations, baptizing them in the name of the Father and of the Son and of the Holy Spirit, <u>and teaching them to obey everything that I have commanded you</u>. And remember, I am with you always, to the end of the age.

<u>Mark</u>

Urgency and elusiveness characterize Mark's presentation of Jesus. The Gospel rushes us into its presentation of "Jesus Christ (or Messiah), Son of God." Even though God acknowledges Jesus as God's own Son (1:11), only twice in the story does anyone else get it. One of those people is the centurion who witnesses Jesus' death (15:39). Many interpreters have noted how often Jesus commands people not to share his wonderful deeds (e.g., 1:41), even telling demons not to announce his identity (3:11-12).

The other person who recognizes Jesus as Messiah is Peter (8:27-33). Even though Peter acknowledges Jesus as the Messiah, he and the other disciples totally fail to understand what that means. Three times, in just three chapters, Jesus tells them the Messiah must suffer before his vindication, and each time they demonstrate their misunderstanding (8:31-33; 9:30-37; 10:32-45).

The disciples' incomprehension provides a likely clue as to why Mark introduces Jesus as the Messiah but people don't recognize him as such. Perhaps people expected a Messiah to rush in, drive out the Romans, restore Israel to prosperity, and reign in glory. Jesus would reign in glory, but only after living through the worst the human condition has to offer – betrayal, injustice, torture, and death. Perhaps, the author of Mark believed no one can understand what it means for Jesus to be the Messiah until they've read the whole story.

Jesus' elusiveness continues all the way through the ending of the Gospel. Mark's Easter story includes no resurrection appearances. Instead, the women are commanded to go tell Peter and the other disciples that Jesus is risen. And the story ends, "So they went out and fled from the tomb, for fear and amazement had seized them; and they said nothing to nobody because they were scared" (16:8, author's translation into Southern). Early Christian copyists, disappointed by this ending, added alternative "happier" endings to Mark, but all of our earliest and best copies of Mark end with the elusive Jesus, out ahead of those who must follow him into the future.

Luke

Luke and Matthew provide stories of Mary's conception and Jesus' infancy; Mark and John do not. If we look carefully, our standard Christmas pageants combine elements from Matthew and Luke, but the two stories are quite different. For example, where astrologers from a royal court pay homage to Jesus in Matthew, Luke sends shepherds. Luke is the Gospel that most embraces humble people and outsiders: the poor, Samaritans, sinners, and women (who were not considered equal to men in the ancient world). It's Luke who tells us about the Good Samaritan, the Prodigal Son, (the rich man and) Lazarus, the (Pharisee and the) Tax Collector, and the Persistent Widow.

In fact, Luke emphasizes Mary far more than Matthew does. Luke's presentation of Mary includes the famous Magnificat, in which Mary celebrates the "great reversal": God scatters the proud, pulls down the mighty, and sends the rich away empty, but God lifts up the lowly and fills the hungry with good things. Luke's Jesus cares deeply about possessions and social status – and how his disciples use them. (Look at Jesus' first teaching session in Luke 4:16-30).

Compare Luke 1:1-4 with Acts 1:1-3, and you'll see that whoever wrote Luke also wrote the book of Acts. That means that Luke's Gospel teaches that the story of Jesus continues in the ongoing life of the church. Luke's ending demonstrates this point. The risen Jesus walks along the road with two of his disciples, but they do not recognize him. It is only when Jesus <u>takes</u> bread, <u>blesses</u> it, <u>breaks</u> it, and <u>gives</u> it to them – signs of the Eucharist! – that their eyes are opened (24:30-31). Through the Holy Spirit

79

Jesus is present with the church, so Luke's Gospel ends where Acts begins, with the promise of the Holy Spirit (24:44-49; see Acts 1:8).

John

The Gospel of John begins with some of the most glorious language in the New Testament. "In the beginning was the Word." Right from the start, it announces that Jesus embodies the very presence of God among mortals. "And the Word became flesh and dwelt among us, full of grace and truth." The Gospel of John testifies to Jesus' oneness with God over and over again.

In fact, at seven key points in John Jesus exclaims, "I AM" the bread of life, the light of the world, the door of the sheep, the good shepherd, the resurrection and the life, the way, the truth, and the life, the true vine. This is no mere accident. These sayings occur only in John's Gospel. By "I AM" Jesus indicates his divine identity; "I AM" is the divine name revealed to Moses in Exodus 3:14. Thus, when the mob comes to arrest Jesus and Jesus asks them whom they seek, his reply – I AM – drives them to the ground. They are in the very presence of God. Seven "signs" (or miracles) point to Jesus' true identity throughout the Gospel.

The problem is, "The light shines in the darkness, and the darkness did not overcome it" (1:5; see 1:10-11). Despite the revelation of God's Word through Jesus, people still do not get it. This explains why people seem not to understand Jesus throughout John's Gospel. Jesus speaks at a heavenly or spiritual level, which their earthly comprehension cannot grasp. Nicodemus does not understand what it means to be born "from above" (3:3-4), the Samaritan Woman is confused by "living water" (4:10-15), and Pilate says more than he knows by labeling Jesus "King of the Jews" (19:19-22). At the end of the story, even Peter fails to understand the teachings of the risen Jesus (21:15-23). Jesus embodies all the blessings of heaven, but people are not prepared to receive him.

John draws toward a conclusion with the appearances of the risen Jesus in chapter 20. Still, that tension between the heavenly Jesus and people's ability to accept him continues. Thomas, who has missed Jesus' earlier encounter with the Risen One, refuses to believe. "Unless I see the mark of the nails in his hands, and put my finger in the mark of the nails and my hand in his side, I will not believe" (20:25). Yet, "full of grace and truth" (1:14) Jesus appears to Thomas and allows Thomas to probe his wounds. "Blessed are those who have not seen and yet have come to believe" (20:29). Indeed, that is why someone wrote this Gospel:

> Now Jesus did many other signs in the presence of his disciples, which are not written in this book. But these are written so that you may come to believe that Jesus is the Messiah, the Son of God, and that through believing you may have life in his name. (20:30-31)

So What?

We have explored how the beginnings and endings of the Gospels reflect their major emphases. Each Gospel has a distinctive beginning and a particular ending, just as each Gospel testifies to Jesus in its own characteristic way.

Some Christians might prefer one Gospel, with one consistent message. However, through the centuries the church has insisted that we're better off with our four Gospels. Each story has its own contribution to add to our churches, to our imaginations, and to our spirits.

We might imagine a musician who has studied with several teachers. We all need consistency. Too many teachers, and a musician's progress will be inconsistent; technique will be spotty. But every musician needs change as well, as each good teacher adds new layers of technique, understanding, and expression. That's why the church values its diverse Gospels; each makes its own contribution to our common life.

APPENDIX

Each Gospel has its own way of presenting Jesus. Many of these "distinctives" can be found in multiple Gospels, but one emphasizes them more than others.

Gospel Distingtives

Matthew	• Jesus as Israel's king • Emphasis on doing what Jesus says • Instructions for the church • Disciples as having "little faith" • Emphasis on final judgment
Mark	• Secret Messiah • Jesus performs the works of God • Disciples don't get it – "no faith" • Jesus in open conflict with the Temple establishment • Mark's open ending

Luke	• Jesus the Savior who restores people to wholeness • Jesus the innocent prophet • The inclusion of outsiders: Samaritans, sinners, women, gentiles • Emphasis on possessions and the poor • Memorable parables: Samaritan, Dishonest Manager, Rich Man and Lazarus, Prodigal Son, Pharisee and the Tax Collector, Widow and the Dishonest Judge • The composition of Acts
John	• Early Christians called it a "spiritual Gospel" • "In the beginning was the Word… and the Word was God" • Jesus talks mostly about himself: seven "I AM" sayings • Miracles as "signs" that reveal Jesus' identity • Jesus' death and resurrection as his glorification

Class Session
Spiritual Practice

Begin class with a time of silence, during which the leader reads Luke 2:41-52. Following the reading of the passage, take time in silence to reflect on what word, image or phrase "speaks" to you today. After a few minutes of silence, share your reflections with the group.

Questions for Discussion:

1. Invite someone in the class to identify a historical figure who has influenced or inspired them . Then ask, Would you prefer to have three biographies of this person, which differed in some particulars, or just one? What would be the advantages and disadvantages of having one? Of having three?

2. Early Christians recognized and affirmed diverse portraits of Jesus. What does their affirmation of diversity say to us in relationship to diversities in Christianity? Is Christian diversity a good thing? Why? If not, how might diversity be a problem?

3. Are you more familiar with one of the Gospels than with the others? Has anyone in the class ever noticed that they have a "favorite" Gospel?

4. Compare the healing stories of the hemorrhaging woman in Mark 5 and Matthew 9. Which version appeals to you most, and why?

5. Invite the class to consider which Gospel beginning they find most inspiring or most interesting. Which ending? Looking at the chart included in the study guide, does one of the Gospels come closest to your own understanding of Christ?

6. The first version of Mark's gospel, according to scholars, ends at Mark 16:8. Take some time to Read Mark 16:1-8. What do you notice about the story? What would your faith be like if that was

the only story of the resurrection? Read Mark 16:9-20. How does this summary of Jesus' post-resurrection appearances expand on the earlier version?

Conclude the session with prayers of gratitude for God's good news in your life. Take time to share where God has made a difference in your life and give thanks for God's presence.

NOTES:

SESSION EIGHT

Gifts of Our Tradition : Church History
Anne Thayer

"Welcome to the Family Reunion!"

Why do we make a special effort to get together with our families from time to time? We share ancestors; we are dealing with the legacy they left us. Often we share the same food, the same jokes, sometimes, the same pain. We want to figure out who goes with whom. We want to catch up; we need to share our stories. Ultimately we want to know better who we are, how we got here, and how to move forward. Similar reasons pertain to studying our church family.

As Christians, God's incarnation among us is a fundamental touchstone of history. We are convinced that God has acted decisively in the world and continues to act among us. Without denying that God is at work anywhere and anytime, we look to the church as the body of Christ, the key locus of God's ongoing activity in the world. We, as believers today, belong to a body of believers with an extensive reach in both time and place. And God has been shaping this body and giving it gifts through the centuries, right up to today. As Rowan Williams, the Archbishop of Canterbury, has written:

> Who I am as a Christian is something which, in theological terms, I could only answer fully on the impossible supposition that I could see and grasp how all other Christian lives had shaped mine and, more specifically,

shaped it towards the likeness of Christ. I don't and can't know the dimensions of this; but if I have read St Paul in I Corinthians carefully I should at least be thinking of my identity as a believer in terms of a whole immeasurable exchange of gifts, known and unknown, by which particular Christian lives are built up, an exchange between the living and the dead.

... for the Christian involved in church history, the sense of recognition, of anxieties in common, becomes a reinforcement of belief in the Church itself as a society whose roots are in something more than historical process as usually understood. There will be in church history strong elements of institutional history, tracing the ins and outs of power games; there will be records of tragedy and betrayal; there will be long moments where we don't really know at all what made our ancestors work. As Christian students, though, we shall always be haunted by something else: to what call is all this a response – faithful, unfaithful, uncomprehending, transfiguring? Can we acknowledge it as our call too? And more to the point, can we see that our immersion in the ways in which they responded becomes part of the way we actually hear the call ourselves in more and more diverse and more and more complete ways? (Williams 27, 30-31)

In church history, we find Christians responding to the challenges of their times. Whatever issue we face in the church and the world, our predecessors in the faith have thought about it before, and we can learn from their insights. How should we read the Bible? Should we spend money on a new building or spend it on poor relief? Should we have children in worship? How do we teach the basics of the faith? What is the relationship between natural science and theology? Why are we suffering? Between whom can marriages be made (and ended)? How should we pray? Can we worship with those who believe differently? What does the pursuit of justice look like?

"How did we end up with the doctrine of the Trinity? I can't really make sense of it..."

Studying the history of the church is very helpful in learning basic Christian teachings and how they came about. It helps us understand people from diverse Christian backgrounds. An early challenge was how to understand Jesus. Was Jesus really God? Was Jesus some kind of intermediate being, less than God but more than human? Was Jesus simply an exemplary human being and great moral teacher?

The earliest followers of Jesus were Jews who worshipped one God; their monotheism made them stand out in the ancient world. And yet, they became convinced that they had encountered this same God in the person of Jesus of Nazareth. Particularly after the events of Jesus' resurrection and Pentecost, they also became convinced that this same God was with them in an ongoing way that they called the Holy Spirit. The understanding of God as Trinity arose out of their vital, personal, and transforming encounters with God.

Many of their gentile contemporaries and fellow converts to Christianity were so convinced of the pure spiritual and unchanging nature of God that they really couldn't stomach the idea of God becoming human. Jesus must not have been fully human – he was just a human façade for the true God who could never be born, get tired, or die. Or, if Jesus was truly human, whatever was divine about him must have been less than God's own divinity. The issue came to a head in the 4th century. A priest from Alexandria in Egypt taught that the divine in Jesus was God's first and best creation, created to be the agent for the creation of the world. While this made sense to many people, ultimately several church councils decided it. The words of the Nicene Creed declare that Jesus Christ was "God from God, light from light, true God from true God, begotten not made, of one being with the Father." Similarly, it was decided that the Holy Spirit was also divine. By the end of the 4th century, the doctrine of the Trinity was established: one God in three persons. Outside of the Bible, the Nicene Creed is the most ecumenical document of Christianity, used by Roman

Catholic, Orthodox and most Protestant Christians.

What was at stake here? While reading the heated debates that led to these decisions is not always edifying, we learn that Christians were affirming that it is God who brings about reconciliation between God and humans. We aren't simply exhorted to follow an example and become like Christ to become children of God. Rather God has taken on human nature and lifted it up to participate in the divine life. We learn that in Jesus and the Holy Spirit we get to know God and experience God's love; we don't simply have messengers separate from God. We learn that God comes to us in personal ways, just as the writers of the New Testament had encountered the one God in Jesus Christ.

Does the doctrine of the Trinity (one God in three persons) "make sense"? Is it fully explainable? For centuries, Christians have acknowledged a sense of mystery at the center of our faith, while using Trinitarian language to name the God they encounter, love and worship. (See Quash and Ward.)

"Well, you know, it used to be easier to be a Christian…"

Depending on where we live, what our personal history has been, there may be a temptation to cast a nostalgic eye on the past. And yet the history of the church gives us striking examples of people who found that the cost of discipleship was high and yet they were willing to pay the cost. Take, for example, Perpetua, a 22-year old Roman wife and mother who was a catechumen in 203. She had come under the influence of the Christians in North Africa where she lived and was taking lessons in preparation for her baptism. The Roman Emperor, Septimius Severus, committed to enhancing traditional Roman religion, issued an edict banning conversion to Judaism or Christianity. Perpetua was arrested; it was made clear to her that if she didn't go through with her baptism she would be released to return to her family and infant son. She recorded her experiences in prison:

> While we were still with the persecutors, and my father, for the sake of his affection for me, was persisting in seeking to turn me away, and to cast me down from the

faith – 'Father,' said I, 'do you see, let us say, this vessel lying here to be a little pitcher, or something else?' And he said, 'I see it to be so.' And I replied to him, 'Can it be called by any other name than what it is?' And he said, 'No.' 'Neither can I call myself anything else than what I am, a Christian' (Perpetua 28).

Perpetua went ahead with her baptism, comforted her fellow Christians in prison, and went to her death in the arena singing psalms, confident that Christ would fight this battle for her. Perpetua's story was circulated widely in the ancient world, giving courage to other Christians facing harassment, persecution or death.

Or again, we might be inspired by the witness of Julia Foote (1823-1900). Born in Schenectady, New York to former slaves who had purchased their freedom, she became convinced that God was calling her to preach. She struggled to get an education in a segregated society, became alienated from her husband who objected to her evangelistic activities, for years was called a schismatic and excommunicated from her church for holding meetings in her home. She also had to overcome her own "doubts and fears." In her autobiography, she wrote, "I had always been opposed to the preaching of women, and had spoken against it, though, I acknowledge, without foundation. This rose before me like a mountain, and when I thought of the difficulties they had to encounter… I shrank back and cried, "Lord, I cannot go!" (Foote 200-201). Yet the call persisted and she took up an itinerant preaching ministry. After being barred from preaching in a Baptist church in Chillicothe, Ohio because she was a woman, and refusing to preach for the Methodists because they would only allow white folks to attend, she reported,

We visited Zanesville, Ohio, laboring for white and colored people…. God the Holy Ghost was powerfully manifest in all these meetings…. Whatever I needed, by faith I had. Glory! Glory!! While God lives, and Jesus sits on his right hand, nothing shall be impossible unto me, if I hold fast faith with a pure conscience" (Foote

221-222).

Years later, Julia Foote became the first woman in the American Methodist Episcopal Zion Church to be ordained a deacon; she also became the second female elder ordained in her denomination.

Such stories remind us that God's claim on our lives is total. They offer a counter-weight to temptations to prioritize our own desires and cultural norms. They remind us that God gives strength to go into unlikely and dangerous places. From the discipleship of the early apostles, to the visions of Hildegard of Bingen, to the trials of Martin Luther, to the service of Mother Teresa, learning about the lives of our predecessors in faith helps us to see the cost and joy of discipleship.

"We've always worshipped this way..."

Well, yes and no. Worship practices have provided the Christian community with a great deal of continuity over the last twenty centuries, and yet we know how contentious it can be to meddle with an order of worship or change a hymnal. In the second century, Justin Martyr explained that Christians worship on Sundays, "inasmuch as it is the first day on which God, transforming the darkness and matter, created the universe; and on the same day our Savior Jesus Christ rose from the dead." In the Sunday gathering, Justin continues, "the memoirs of the apostles or the writings of the prophets are read... the president, in a discourse admonishes and invites the people to practice these examples of virtue. Then we all stand up together and offer prayers... bread is presented, and wine with water; the president likewise offers up prayers and thanksgivings according to his ability, and the people assent by saying, Amen. The elements which have been 'eucharistized' are distributed and received by each one" (Thompson 8-9). This sounds very familiar: scripture, sermon, prayers, communion. Other early church sources record the use of prayers that are still in widespread use:

The Lord be with you.
And with your spirit.

Lift up your hearts.
> We lift them up to the Lord.
Let us give thanks to the Lord.
> It is meet and right so to do.

A thousand years later in western Europe, most of these elements were still in use, although the liturgy had become more elaborate, leaving little freedom for the celebrant to use his own words. Further, the liturgy remained in Latin, the old language, rather than the languages contemporary people spoke. Although sermons were preached, they were unlikely to have been heard every Sunday in most parishes; the eucharist was the sine qua non of Sunday worship. Those in the congregation were urged to say their prayers along with those of the priest in the drama of the mass. While priests took communion every time they celebrated mass, lay worshippers were expected to participate spiritually, by seeing the consecrated host, every week, but only to physically receive the host once a year on Easter.

At the time of the Protestant Reformation, many felt that worship services needed to be drastically revised. The preaching of the Bible came to be the centerpiece of Protestant worship. Services were conducted in the vernacular; people were told to stop saying their own prayers throughout the service and instead listen to the pastor. Many "ceremonies," seen as human accretions onto godly worship, were simplified or removed altogether. Some, such as the Anabaptists, eschewed a formal liturgy. Other groups, such as Anglicans and Lutherans retained a set liturgy. Across the board, the nature of Christ's presence in sacraments and community was vigorously contested. (See Thompson.)

Among Protestants, congregational singing was given a central place. But what should be sung? Luther wrote many hymns. Sometimes he composed both words and music, sometimes he took existing popular tunes (such as drinking songs) and put new words to them. Calvin limited singing to the Psalter, the Biblical songbook, but had tunes written that would highlight the words through dignified melodies. Singing often spilled over into personal devotion. Katherine Schütz Zell, a lay reformer in sixteenth-century Strasbourg, wrote in a preface to a hymnal, "Therefore now let us sing these songs, which express so admirably God's love toward us and exhort us so faithfully not to neglect the salvation offered to us" (Zell 94).

As Christianity has taken root in more and more cultures over time, worship has both reflected and shaped local sensibilities. In the orthodox traditions of the East, liturgy has long been experienced as a foretaste of heaven and a source of revelation here on earth. Icons provide windows onto spiritual reality and the rhythm of fasting and feasting has deepened Christians' spiritual engagement. Chinese liturgical sutras were composed in the 8th century, addressing God as the "radiant Jade-faced One." In Mexico in the 17th century, popular folk tunes and African dance rhythms made their way into liturgical music, with popular pieces often drawing in great crowds. In southern India in the late 20th century, James Appavoo created Tamil Christian music in Dalit musical style, drawing heavily on the folk culture of the majority of Protestant Christians there. All around the globe, the use of local music, visual arts, drama, and rhetorical styles all contribute to the establishment of the gospel. As any congregation seeks to evaluate, expand or change its worship, a study of the ways Christians have worshipped offers guidance on key features of one's own tradition as well as encouraging a freedom to try new expressions.

"Let's not do that again!"

George Santayana's aphorism is often repeated, "Those who cannot remember the past are condemned to repeat it." Not every chapter of the history of the Church has been inspiring; just because we've done it before does not mean we ought to do it again. Church history offers some cautionary tales. The Crusades are often lifted up as one of the key failures of the western church. While there was great enthusiasm among Europeans for the Crusades in the Middle Ages, the long term evaluation of the church has been that they did more harm than good.

The Crusades were a series of military expeditions designed to ensure Christian access to pilgrimage sites in the Holy Land. Tied in with the penitential spirituality of the day, crusades involved liturgies, processions, fasts and prayers, along with military action. Pope Urban II (1088-1099) preached the first Crusade at the Council of Clermont in 1095, urging Christians to liberate Jerusalem from infidel hands and to aid beleaguered Eastern Christians. Jerusalem was captured in 1099, and there was a Christian political state in the Holy Land until 1291. Subsequent crusades were less successful. Violence expanded in the Crusaders' wake, targeting Jews along with Muslims. Crusaders often failed to see Eastern Christians as fellow believers, and the 4th Crusade gained notoriety by attacking Constantinople, the Christian capital of the East. The magnificent church of Hagia Sophia was desecrated and ransacked. Although some questioned the wisdom of crusading as a Christian undertaking at the time, most interpreted the crusaders' success as divine approbation and failure as divine displeasure over sin.

In the long run, the Crusades left a bitter legacy. Christians did get freer access to pilgrimage sites, and the reigning assumption that the monastic life was more spiritually valuable than Christian life in society was profoundly challenged. Yet, relationships between eastern and western Christians are still ruptured. Christians living in Muslim lands suffered for the deeds of western Christians. Among many Muslims, distrust of Christians has proved long-lasting. The situation of the Jews in Europe declined drastically, as vengeance for Christ led to violence at home as well as abroad. In the later Middle Ages, Jews were expelled from western Europe and moved east, setting up the demographics that met with the horrors of the Holocaust. On the economic and cultural fronts, new trade opportunities and ancient text preserved in Arabic became available to the West. The significance of these is debated; historian Jacques Le Goff claims that "the apricot" was the only advantage Europe gained. Thus, when the word "crusade" is used today, it may mean a cause pursued with great vigor, such as a "crusade against homelessness." But it also carries a dark side of misdirected religiously-inspired violence.

"Seek the Lord…"

Throughout the history of the church, Christians have cultivated deep spiritual lives and produced a treasure trove of devotional resources. These texts and models are available to us even as we adapt them to our contemporary settings.

In the fourth century, men and women took to the deserts of Egypt and Palestine to pray, fast and practice other spiritual disciplines. The sayings of those who gained a reputation for wisdom were collected for others to meditate upon. As you struggle with temptation, consider the words of Abba Hyperichius, "Keep praising God with hymns, and meditating continually, and so lighten the burden of the temptations that attack you. A traveler carrying a heavy burden stops from time to time to take deep breaths, and so makes the journey easier and the burden light" (Ward 65). Or the words of Amma Syncletica, "An open treasury is quickly spent; any virtue will be lost if it is published abroad and is known about everywhere. If you put wax in front of a fire it melts; and if you pour vain praises on the soul it goes soft and weak in seeking goodness" (Ward 82).

St. Benedict's famous Rule, written in the 6th century, ordered the lives of monks and nuns, giving them time each day for prayer, labor, food, and rest. While the thoroughgoing dedication of such people may seem out of reach, many of their spiritual practices are not. Many Christians punctuate their days with prayer, pausing morning and evening to read a short passage of scripture, offer prayers, and reflect on the day. Lectio divina is a style of reading in this tradition that listens for God's voice through slow and meditative reading, followed by prayer in response. The Benedictine model of spirituality encourages a balance of activities, as well as a hefty dose of silence. The many writings in the monastic traditions, ancient and modern, continue to nurture thirsty spirits.

In fact, many famous spiritual writers report that they were greatly aided by reading the writings of others. For instance, Teresa of Avila wrote that she was very impressed by St. Augustine's Confessions:

> I was given St. Augustine's Confessions, seemingly by the ordainment of the Lord.... When I began to read the Confessions I seemed to see myself portrayed there ... When I came to the tale of his conversion, and heard how he heard the voice in the garden, it seemed exactly as if the Lord had spoken to me. So I felt in my heart. For some time I was dissolved in tears, in great inward affliction and distress... I believe that my soul gained great strength from His Divine Majesty, and that He must have heard my lamentations and taken pity on all my tears. A desire to spend more time with Him began to grow in me (Teresa 69).

Along with spiritual narratives and guidance, books of prayers and hymns are available to us from all across the body of Christ. Think for a moment about where your Christmas and Easter hymns have come from. Many hymnals include words penned by ancient, medieval and modern writers. Some of our "old favorites" are only a century or two old; some are nearly twenty centuries old. Our predecessors in faith have prayed to God in many ways, some spontaneous, some learned by heart, many recorded for our use. Especially when we pray together, the language of prayer draws on our historical memory and employs the gifts of the body of Christ.

And so, Welcome to the Family Reunion! So glad you came! We have so much to catch up on ...

Class Session

Spiritual Practice

As you prepare to study together, quiet your heart and listen as the leader reads Act 17:16-28. After a few minutes of silence, during which you meditate on any words, images or phrases that have come to you in light of the scripture, share your thoughts with the group.

Questions for Discussion:

1. Name some of the "traditions" that are important to your church family and give you a united identity. Consider a few of the questions presented by the author in the opening paragraphs of her essay.

2. What is your understanding of the Doctrine of the Trinity? Does it play an important role in your faith and piety? How do you describe its importance to someone outside your church context? Is there room for diversity in our understanding of the Trinity and other doctrines?

3. As you look at your church, what are your constants in worship? What has recently changed in worship? What worship practices might deepen your congregation's life? How do you best join tradition and novelty in worship?

4. Storytelling is part of life and our history. What stories have you heard about your church's history? What were the high points? What was humorous? What might have been tragic?

5. In what ways is it "easy" for you to live within God's claim on your life? What are situations and ideas that stretch you when you consider God's claim on your life?

6. Assuming there may be a breadth of experience in the group:

- Describe worship in your church 50+ years ago (kinds of hymnals, songs, instruments; who led worship; how did people dress, act, etc.)
- Describe worship in your church today.

What do you miss or mourn? What do you celebrate? How has

your past informed your current practices? How might you be building a future on today's foundation?

In conclusion, take time to note the important people in your church's history. Give thanks for their commitment to God.

Works Cited

Foote, Julia A. J. "A Brand Plucked from the Fire." Sisters of the Spirit: Three Black Women's Autobiographies of the Nineteenth Century. Ed. William L. Andrews. Bloomington: Indiana University Press, 1986.

Perpetua. "The Martyrdom of Perpetua." In Her Words: Women's Writings in the History of Christian Thought. Ed. Amy Oden. Nashville: Abingdon Press, 1994. 26-37.

Quash, Ben and Michael Ward, eds. Heresies and How to Avoid Them: Why It Matters What Christians Believe. Peabody, MA: Hendrickson Publishers, 2007.

Ripley, Dorothy. "An Account of the Extraordinary Conversion and Religious Experience of Dorothy Ripley." Her Own Story: Autobiographical Portraits of Early Methodist Women. Ed. Paul Wesley Chilcote. Nashville: Kingswood Books, 2001.

Teresa of Avila. The Life of Saint Teresa of Avila by Herself. London: Penguin Books, 1957.

Thompson, Bard, ed. Liturgies of the Western Church. Philadelphia: Fortress Press, 1961.

Ward, Benedicta. The Desert Fathers: Sayings of the Early Christian Monks. London: Penguin Books, 2003.

Williams, Rowan. Why Study the Past? The Quest for the Historical Church. Grand Rapids: Eerdmans, 2005.

Zell, Katharina Schütz. Church Mother: The Writings of a Protestant Reformers in Sixteenth-Century Germany. Ed. and trans. Elsie McKee. Chicago: University of Chicago Press, 2006.

NOTES:

LaVergne, TN USA
09 March 2011

219336LV00002B/7/P